Alastair
Sawday's

Special Places
to Stay

Briti
Hotel Inns

"Filled the characterful
detail love from the
Sawd eam."
The L ng Standard

ipa
Publisher
of the Year

Edited

's

Breakfast

"Exceptional places to stay."
The Daily Telegraph

Edited by Nicola Crosse

ipa
Publisher
of the Year

Sawday's

Places

& Inns
& Wales

" teed to cheer
the traveller."
Food & Travel Magazine

Edited by David Hancock

Alastair
Sawday's

Special Places
to Stay

British Bed & Breakfast
for Garden Lovers

"The ideal all-round
publication for a gardener's
weekend away"
The Times

Edited by Nicola Crosse

Alastair
Sawday's

Special Places to St

First edition

Copyright © 2010 Alastair Sawday
Publishing Co. Ltd
Published in June 2010
ISBN-13: 978-1-906136-34-5

Alastair Sawday Publishing Co. Ltd,
The Old Farmyard, Yanley Lane,
Long Ashton, Bristol BS41 9LR, UK
Tel: +44 (0)1275 395430
Email: info@sawdays.co.uk
Web: www.sawdays.co.uk

The Globe Pequot Press,
P. O. Box 480, Guilford,
Connecticut 06437, USA
Tel: +1 203 458 4500
Email: info@globepequot.com
Web: www.globepequot.com

*We have made every effort to ensure the accuracy
of the information in this book at the time of
going to press. However, we cannot accept any
responsibility for any loss, injury or
inconvenience resulting from the use of
information contained therein.*

Series Editor Alastair Sawday
Editor Kathie Burton
Editorial Director Annie Shillito
Writing Georgina Black, Carmen Cox,
Viv Cripps, Monica Guy, Honor Peters,
Helen Pickles, Claire Wilson
Inspections Jan Adam, David Ashby,
Neil Brown, Kathie Burton,
Angie Collings, Carmen Cox, Jane Elliot,
Auriol Marson, Scott Reeve,
Mandy Wragg
*Thanks to those people who did a few inspections
or write-ups*
Accounts Bridget Bishop,
Shona Adcock, Rebecca Bebbington,
Christine Buxton, Amy Lancastle,
Sally Ranahan
Editorial Sue Bourner, Jo Boissevain,
Carmen Cox, Nicola Crosse,
Wendy Ogden, Lianka Varga
Production Jules Richardson,
Rachel Coe, Tom Germain,
Anny Mortada
Sales & Marketing & PR Rob Richardson,
Sarah Bolton, Bethan Riach, Lisa Walklin
Web & IT Dominic Oakley
Chris Banks, Phil Clarke,
Mike Peake, Russell Wilkinson.

Alastair Sawday has asserted his right to
be identified as the author of this work

Maps: Maidenhead Cartographic Services
Printing: Butler, Tanner & Dennis, Frome
UK distribution: Penguin UK, London

Alastair Sawday's

Special Places

Venues
in Britain

4 Contents

The buildings

Beautiful as they were, our old offices leaked heat, used electricity to heat water and rooms, flooded spaces with light to illuminate one person, and were not ours to alter.

So in 2005 we created our own eco-offices by converting some old barns to create a low-emissions building. We made the building energy-efficient through a variety of innovative and energy-saving building techniques, described below.

Insulation We went to great lengths to ensure that very little heat can escape, by laying thick insulating board under the roof and floor and adding further insulation underneath the roof and between the rafters. We then lined the whole of the inside of the building with plastic sheeting to ensure air-tightness.

Heating We installed a wood-pellet boiler from Austria, in order to be largely fossil-fuel free. The pellets are made from compressed sawdust, a waste product from timber mills that work only with sustainably managed forests. The heat is conveyed by water, throughout the building, via an under-floor system.

Water We installed a 6000-litre tank to collect rainwater from the roofs. This is pumped back, via an ultra-violet filter, to the lavatories, showers and basins. There are two solar thermal panels on the roof providing heat to the one (massively insulated) hot-water cylinder.

Photo: Tom Germain

Lighting We have a carefully planned mix of low-energy lighting: task lighting and up-lighting. We also installed sun-pipes to reflect the outside light into the building.

Electricity All our electricity has long come from the Good Energy company and is 100% renewable.

Materials Virtually all materials are non-toxic or natural. Our carpets are made from (80%) Herdwick sheep-wool from National Trust farms in the Lake District.

Doors and windows Outside doors and new windows are wooden, double-glazed and beautifully constructed in Norway. Old windows have been double-glazed.

We have a building we are proud of, and architects and designers are fascinated by. But best of all, we are now in a better position to encourage our owners and readers to take sustainability more seriously.

What we do

Besides having moved the business to a low-carbon building, the company works in a number of ways to reduce its overall environmental footprint.

Our footprint We measure our footprint annually and use it to find ways of reducing our environmental impact. To help address unavoidable carbon emissions we try to put something back: since 2006 we have supported SCAD, an organisation that works with villagers in India to create sustainable development.

Travel Staff are encouraged to car-share or cycle to work and we provide showers (rainwater-fed) and bike sheds. Our company cars run on LPG (liquid petroleum gas) or recycled cooking oil. We avoid flying and take the train for business trips wherever possible. All office travel is logged as part of our footprint and we count our freelance editors' and inspectors' miles too.

Our office Nearly all of our office waste is recycled; kitchen waste is composted and used in the office vegetable garden. Organic and fairtrade basic provisions are used in the staff kitchen and at in-house events, and green cleaning products are used throughout the office.

Working with owners We are proud that many of our Special Places help support their local economy and, through our Ethical Collection, we recognise owners who go the extra mile to serve locally sourced and organic food or those who have a positive impact on their environment or community.

Engaging readers We hope to raise awareness of the need for individuals to play their part; our Go Slow series places an emphasis on ethical travel and the Fragile Earth imprint consists of hard-hitting environmental titles. Our Ethical Collection informs readers about owners' ethical endeavours.

Ethical printing We print our books locally to support the British printing industry and to reduce our carbon footprint. We print our books on either FSC-certified or recycled paper, using vegetable or soy-based inks.

Our supply chain Our electricity is 100% renewable (supplied by Good Energy), and we put our savings with Triodos, a bank whose motives we trust. Most supplies are bought in bulk from a local ethical-trading co-operative.

For many years Alastair Sawday Publishing has been 'greening' the business in different ways. Our aim is to reduce our environmental footprint as far as possible, and almost every decision we make takes into account the environmental implications. In recognition of our efforts we won a Business Commitment to the Environment Award in 2005, and in 2006 a Queen's Award for Enterprise in the Sustainable Development category. In that year Alastair was voted ITN's 'Eco Hero'. In 2009 we were given the South West C+ Carbon Positive Consumer Choices Award for our Ethical Collection.

In 2008 and again in 2009 we won the Independent Publishers Guild Environmental Award. In 2009 we were also the IPG overall Independent Publisher and Trade Publisher of the Year. The judging panel were effusive in their praise, stating: "With green issues currently at the forefront of publishers' minds, Alastair Sawday Publishing was singled out in this category as a model for all independents to follow. Its efforts to reduce waste in its office and supply chain have reduced the company's environmental impact, and it works closely with staff to identify more areas of improvement. Here is a publisher who lives and breathes green. Alastair Sawday has all the right principles and is clearly committed to improving its practice further."

Becoming 'green' is a journey and, although we began long before most companies, we still have a long way to go. We don't plan to pursue growth for growth's sake. The Sawday's name – and thus our future – depends on maintaining our integrity. We promote special places – those that add beauty, authenticity and a touch of humanity to our lives. This is a niche, albeit a growing one, so we will spend time pursuing truly special places rather than chasing the mass market.

That said, we do plan to produce more titles as well as to diversify. We are expanding our Go Slow series to other European countries, and have launched *Green Europe*, both bold new publishing projects designed to raise the profile of low-impact tourism. Our Fragile Earth series is a growing collection of campaigning books about the environment: highlighting the perilous state of the world yet offering imaginative and radical solutions and some intriguing facts, these books will keep you up to date and well-armed for the battle with apathy.

Photos: Tom Germain

What to call a book about special places to meet – and to wed, play, think and carouse? We chewed over dozens of options, and still ended up with 'Venues'. But don't let the word conjure images of men in suits and fixed opinions. This is a book about so much more: beauty, idiosyncrasy, character, eclecticism, surprises and lavish attention to good human contact.

So – this is a book about wonderful places to BE.

It is also the beginning of a modest revolution. We reject those cavernous hotel 'catering suites', where the smiles are professional and the system has been tested to distraction by accountants. The carpets swirl or pitter-patter, the staff seem to have come in off the street and the food is meanly portioned. The very word 'banquet' fills me with dread. So we are now doing to 'venues' what we have done to B&Bs: we are widening the definition and celebrating those with panache, style and humanity – and those that dare to be different.

The idea for 'Venues' was born in a B&B, to which a group of us had gone to discuss company strategy. After a cosy and nourishing afternoon in front of the fire, with tea and homemade cakes, and then a glass of wine with our hosts, I realised that meetings (and weddings, parties, dinners etc) could be as varied and as human as nights spent in B&Bs - and as much fun. Then this year we

'threw' a Gathering for our B&B owners here in Bristol, and made our own 'venue' by erecting a marquee on the dockside.

But perhaps we should have tried harder to find a place. We are doing it now, here. Within these pages you will find farms, a windmill, castles, boats, churches, yurts and tipis, art galleries, retreats, restaurants, manor houses and more – there is even a 16th-century tower for the hermitic among you. You can find outrageous luxury, daunting grandeur, stunning style, exquisitely green ways of doing things, organic food, grand Elizabethan clutter, gardens to dream of, simplicity and sophistication, and – above all, some wonderful and imaginative people. For it is the people that make the places what they are.

Alastair Sawday

When Alastair first broached the idea of producing a brand new guide on special places to hold weddings, parties, meetings and conferences, I was immediately enthusiastic. During my pre-Sawday's careers I had both attended and helped to organise numerous meetings and conferences and had more experience of the good, the bad and the frankly indifferent than I care to mention. As for weddings and parties, I've been to a fair few of them in my time and found out, sometimes the hard way, what works and what doesn't. I was lucky enough too to be surrounded by wedding planning whilst in the throes of researching suitable places – my eldest son popped the question and he and his bride-to-be were organising like mad, as were three of my colleagues.

So, feeling suitably primed, I set to thinking about what the key things are

one needs to think about beforehand to make any event really work, and I came up with the following list – in no particular order.

• What type of event are you holding and is the venue able to offer what you need? Helpful at this point to differentiate between your 'must-haves' and your 'nice-to-haves'.

• Choose the right sort of place for the atmosphere you want to create – for a wedding, do you want it to be relaxed and informal or formal and structured? Or you might be looking for somewhere smart, with all comforts and gadgetry laid on, for a business awayday session during the week, followed by a get-in-touch-with-nature weekend with your yoga group, or a big house for a family get-together for Granny's 80th!

• Is location important to you, or is getting exactly the right place higher on your list of priorities?

• How many guests do you plan to have and how do your needs influence the number of spaces and room layouts that you will need?

• How much are you able to spend? Each event will be different, but it's helpful to think about whether you're in the low, medium or high price range. (See Price Bands on page 20 for further details).

Photo left: Ballochneck, entry 167
Photo right: fforest, entry 150

• What about the food and drink? Have a think about what you might like early on. If you're organising a wedding, do you want to leave it all in the hands of the venue or do you want to be more involved in the planning and the sourcing? If you're having a house party, will you do the cooking yourselves or would you like it to be prepared for you?

• How many of you will want to stay at the venue, and how long for? Do you want to be cosseted or are you happy to self-cater?

I hope that this guide helps you to answer all these questions, and that you'll enjoy using it as much as I've enjoyed putting it together – I look forward to getting your feedback.

As for all those weddings – three gloriously happy days have been and gone and we have one more taking place shortly – at one of the venues in this guide of course!

Kathie Burton

Photo: Cadhay, entry 50

It's simple. There are no rules, no boxes to tick. We choose places that we like and are fiercely subjective in our choices. We also recognise that individual requirements will vary and that one person's idea of special is not necessarily someone else's, so there is a huge variety of places, and prices, in the book. Those who are familiar with our Special Places series know that we look for originality and authenticity, and reject the insincere, the anonymous and the banal. The way guests are treated comes as high on our list as the setting, the architecture, the atmosphere and the food.

Inspections

We visit every place in the guide to get a feel for how both the venue and owner or management team tick. We don't have a list of what is acceptable and what is not, but we do meet the owner or the person who manages events and have a good look round. We look for people and places with warmth and personality, combined with professionalism. We want everything to go smoothly on the day, regardless of whether you're organising a small meeting or a huge wedding. It's all fairly informal, but it gives us an excellent idea of who would enjoy holding an event there. Our write-ups are designed to reflect all of these things, so that it helps you to narrow down your choices. Once in the guide, properties are re-inspected every few years, so that we can keep things fresh and accurate.

Photo: Pentillie Castle, entry 27

Feedback

We rely on feedback from our army of readers, as well as from staff members who are encouraged to visit properties across the series. This feedback is invaluable to us and we always follow up on comments. So do tell us whether your event has been a joy or not, if the atmosphere was great or stuffy, the owners and staff cheery or bored. The accuracy of the guide depends on what you, and our inspectors, tell us. A lot of the new entries in each edition are recommended by our readers, so do please tell us about new places you've discovered too. Please use the forms on our website at www.sawdays.co.uk. However, please tell the owner or manager, immediately, about any problems that arise during your event and get them to do something about it there and then. Most owners and staff are more than happy to correct problems and will bend over backwards to help. Far better than bottling it up and then writing to us a week later!

Subscriptions

Owners pay to appear in this guide. Their fee goes towards the high costs of inspecting, of maintaining our website and of producing an all-colour book. We only include places that we find special for one reason or another, so it is not possible for anyone to buy their way onto these pages. Nor is it possible for owners to write their own description. We tell it as we find it and do our best to avoid misleading people.

Disclaimer

We make no claims to pure objectivity in choosing these places. They are here simply because we like them. Our opinions and tastes are ours alone and this book is a statement of them; we hope you will share them. We have done our utmost to get our facts right but apologise unreservedly for any mistakes that may have crept in. The latest information we have about each place can be found on our website, www.sawdays.co.uk, from where you can also click through to the place's website for further details. You should know that we don't check such things as fire alarms, swimming pool security or any other regulation with which owners of properties receiving paying guests should comply. This is the responsibility of the owners.

Photo left: River Cottage HQ, entry 54
Photo right: Cley Windmill, entry 90

Finding the right place for you

All these places are special in one way or another. All have been visited and then written about honestly so that you can find what you want and leave the rest. Those of you who swear by Sawday's books trust our write-ups precisely because we don't have a blanket standard; we include places simply because we like them. But we all have different priorities, so do read the descriptions carefully and pick out the places which might suit you and the type of event you are planning to hold. It is not possible for us to list all the options available at each place, so do follow this up with a visit to the venue's website, and/or a phone call for further information. If something is particularly important to you then do check when you first make enquiries: a simple question or two can often clarify whether somewhere is suitable or not.

Photo: Boconnoc, entry 25

Maps

Each property is flagged with its entry number on the maps at the front. These maps are a great starting point for planning, but please don't use them as anything other than a general guide – use a decent road map for real navigation. Most places will have detailed directions on their website or will be happy to send them once you have made an enquiry.

Ethical Collection

We're always keen to draw attention to places which are striving to have a positive impact on the world, so you'll notice that some entries are flagged as being part of our 'Ethical Collection'. These places are working hard to reduce their environmental footprint, making significant contributions to their local community, or are passionate about serving local or organic food. Owners or managers have had to fill in a very detailed questionnaire before becoming part of this Collection – read more on page 208. This doesn't mean that other places in the guide are not taking similar initiatives – many are – but we may not yet know about them.

Symbols

Below each entry you will see some symbols, which are explained on the back page of the book. They are based on the information given to us by the owners. However, things do change, so please use the symbols as a guide rather than an absolute statement of fact and double-check anything that is important to you – owners occasionally bend their own rules, so it's worth asking for something you'd particularly like, even if they don't have the symbol.

Wheelchair access – some places are keen to accept wheelchair users into their places and have made provision for them. See the quick reference indices at the back of the guide for a list of these.

Our wheelchair symbol indicates that as a minimum there will be access to some public rooms and to WCs. However, this does not mean that wheelchair users will always be met with a perfect landscape. You may encounter ramps, a shallow step, gravelled paths or alternative routes into some rooms. In short, there may be the odd hindrance and we urge you to call and make sure you will get what you need…

Photo: Chalice Hill House, entry 117

Types of places

Venues vary from the small and intimate to the grand and stately; from the simple and charming to the luxurious, as well as the quirky and the unusual. Options may be limited in some to a room or two in which to hold meetings or small parties; in others there will be a wide selection of spaces in which to gather. Many will either own or be able to hire a marquee and some will even be able to offer the option of a tipi or yurt in the grounds. Some will hold the full range of events, ie weddings, parties, meetings and conferences and others will limit themselves to one or two activities. Some places can hire individual spaces by the day, others will expect you to book the whole place for exclusive use, sometimes including bedrooms if they have them. In that case the minimum stay would normally be two nights, particularly for house-party bookings, but do check with the venue.

Definitions of activities

'Weddings' also covers civil ceremonies; if a wedding venue does not have a licence to hold the ceremony itself we will say so. 'Parties' covers both one-off events such as a lunch, dinner or larger gathering, as well as house parties (often self-catered but some places can provide a chef or meals to order). As a rough guide, 'Meetings' cover business gatherings of up to 50 people, 'conferences' anything above that number. This will sometimes include accommodation, but many places can be

used for one-day events too. Some are also able to offer outdoor or team-building activities (see the quick references indices at the back of the book for these and for lists of house-party venues).

Event Spaces

The guide specifies the total number of spaces at the venue that can be used for an event at the venue, plus marquees or perhaps a yurt or tipi, and the maximum number of guests who can be accommodated in each type of room layout in a single space (including a marquee where shown). These room layouts are described as 'Board' (a single large table, suitable for a formal business meeting or dinner party); Cabaret (individual tables, often round and seating up to 10 – the most usual layout for a wedding 'breakfast', ie the meal after the ceremony has taken place, regardless of time of day); Theatre (rows of seats with one or more aisles between, often used for a wedding ceremony or conference); and Reception (for stand-up parties, usually either with drinks and nibbles, or with buffet meals).

The 'Sleeps' field in the guide indicates the maximum number of people (excluding extra beds for children) who can sleep at the venue or in adjacent accommodation under the same ownership. We specify whether this is on a bed and breakfast (B&B), dinner, bed and breakfast (DB&B), self-catering

(S/C) or catered basis, or a combination of these. Please note that not all of the venues have on-site accommodation – do visit our website www.sawdays.co.uk to find one of our 'special places to stay' nearby.

Catering

We specify where guests must use the in-house team, or choose from a list of approved caterers. 'Own caterers' means that guests are allowed to self cater or bring their own caterers.

Price bands

Most of the places in this guide will tailor an event to suit the needs of the party, making it very difficult to list specific prices. We have included a price guideline from £ to £££££ to indicate where each venue sits in relation to others in the guide. Standards and services available will vary accordingly.

See the quick reference section at the back of the book for a breakdown of low, medium and high priced venues.

Closed

When given in months this means for the whole of the month stated. So, 'Closed: November–March' means closed from 1 November to 31 March.

Your requirements

Check from what time the venue will be available and when you will be expected to depart, and what will be included and what you will need to organise yourself. Please try to give as much information about your requirements as you can at the time of your original enquiry, as this will avoid misunderstandings and help to ensure that you get exactly what you want from your event. Ask for a written quote and for details of their cancellation policy.

Photo: Brunel's ss Great Britain, entry 7

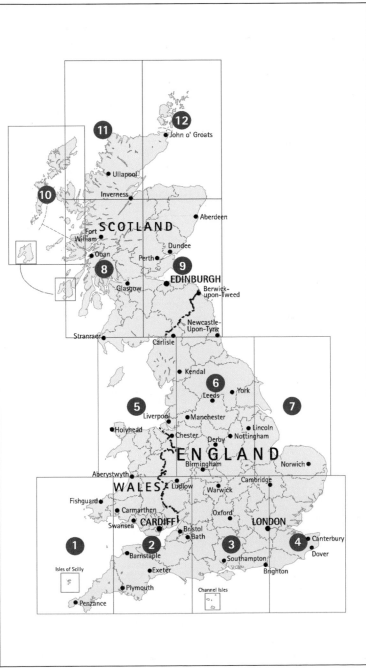

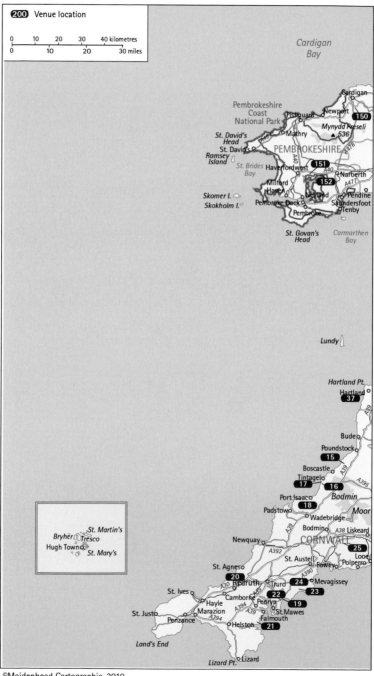

200 Venue location

0 10 20 30 40 kilometres
0 10 20 30 miles

Cardigan Bay

Pembrokeshire Coast National Park

St. David's Head
St. David's
Ramsey Island
St. Brides Bay
Skomer I.
Skokholm I.

Fishguard
Mathry
Newport
Mynydd Preseli ▲ 536
Cardigan

150

PEMBROKESHIRE

Haverfordwest
151
Narberth

Milford Haven
152
Neyland
Pendine

Pembroke Dock
Pembroke
Saundersfoot
Tenby

St. Govan's Head
Carmarthen Bay

Lundy

Hartland Pt.
Hartland
37

Bude
Poundstock
15

Boscastle
Tintagel
17　**16**

Port Isaac
18
Padstow
Wadebridge
Bodmin
Bodmin Moor
Liskeard
25

Newquay
St. Austell
Looe
Fowey
Polperro

St. Agnes
20
Redruth
Truro
24
Mevagissey
23

St. Ives
Camborne
Penryn
22
19

Hayle
Marazion
St. Mawes

St. Just
Penzance
Falmouth
21

Helston

Land's End

Lizard Pt.
Lizard

CORNWALL

St. Martin's
Bryher
Tresco
Hugh Town
St. Mary's

Map 2   23

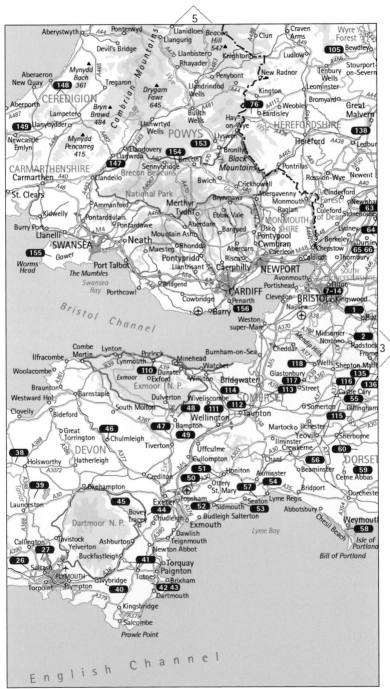

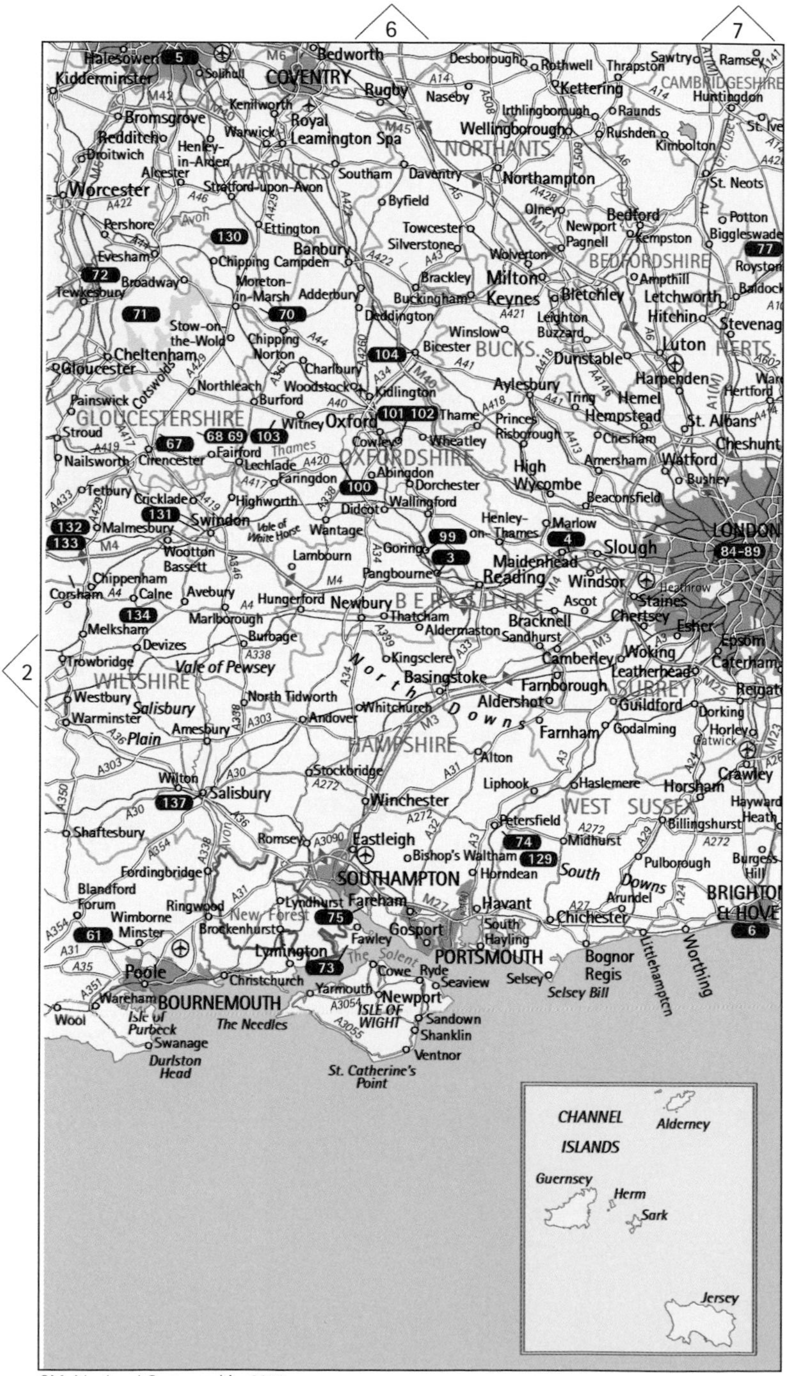
6
7
2
Halesowen
Kidderminster
Solihull
M6
Bedworth
COVENTRY
Desborough
Rothwell
Thrapston
Sawtry
Ramsey
Rugby
Naseby
Kettering
CAMBRIDGESHIRE
Huntingdon
Bromsgrove
Kenilworth
Royal
Leamington Spa
Irthlingborough
Raunds
Redditch
Warwick
M45
Wellingborough
Rushden
St. Ives
Droitwich
Henley-
in-Arden
NORTHANTS
Kimbolton
Alcester
WARWICKS
Southam
Daventry
Northampton
Worcester
Stratford-upon-Avon
St. Neots
A422
A46
Byfield
A428
Olney
Bedford
Pershore
Avon
Ettington
Towcester
Newport
Pagnell
Kempston
Potton
Biggleswade
130
Banbury
Silverstone
77
Evesham
Chipping Campden
A422
A43
Wolverton
BEDFORDSHIRE
Royston
72
Broadway
Moreton-
in-Marsh
Adderbury
Brackley
Milton
Keynes
Ampthill
Baldock
Tewkesbury
Buckingham
Bletchley
Letchworth
71
70
Deddington
A421
Leighton
Buzzard
Hitchin
Stevenage
Stow-on-
the-Wold
Chipping
Norton
Winslow
Cheltenham
104
Bicester
BUCKS.
Luton
HERTS.
Gloucester
Charlbury
A41
Dunstable
Harpenden
Cotswolds
Northleach
Woodstock
Kidlington
Aylesbury
Hertford
Painswick
Burford
A40
Tring
Hemel
Hempstead
GLOUCESTERSHIRE
101
102
Thame
Princes
Risborough
St. Albans
Stroud
Witney
Oxford
A419
67
68
69
103
Thames
Cowley
Wheatley
Chesham
Cheshunt
Nailsworth
Cirencester
Fairford
Lechlade
A420
OXFORDSHIRE
High
Wycombe
Amersham
Watford
Faringdon
Abingdon
Bushey
Tetbury
100
Dorchester
Cricklade
Highworth
Wallingford
Beaconsfield
131
Swindon
Didcot
Henley-
on-Thames
Marlow
132
Malmesbury
Vale of
White Horse
Wantage
99
4
LONDON
133
M4
Wootton
Bassett
Lambourn
Goring
3
Maidenhead
Slough
84-89
Pangbourne
Chippenham
M4
Reading
Windsor
Heathrow
Corsham
A4
Calne
Avebury
A4
Hungerford
Newbury
BERKSHIRE
Ascot
Staines
134
Marlborough
Thatcham
Aldermaston
Bracknell
Chertsey
Esher
Melksham
Burbage
Sandhurst
Epsom
Devizes
A338
M3
Trowbridge
Vale of Pewsey
North
Kingsclere
Camberley
Woking
Caterham
WILTSHIRE
Basingstoke
Leatherhead
Farnborough
SURREY
Reigate
Westbury
North Tidworth
Aldershot
Salisbury
Plain
Whitchurch
Downs
Guildford
Dorking
Warminster
A303
Andover
M3
Amesbury
Farnham
Godalming
Horley
Gatwick
HAMPSHIRE
Alton
A303
A30
Stockbridge
A31
Crawley
Wilton
Liphook
Haslemere
Horsham
137
Salisbury
A272
Winchester
WEST SUSSEX
Hayward
Heath
Shaftesbury
A30
A272
Petersfield
Billingshurst
A272
Romsey
A3090
Eastleigh
74
Midhurst
A354
Bishop's Waltham
129
Pulborough
Burgess
Hill
Fordingbridge
SOUTHAMPTON
Horndean
South
Downs
BRIGHTON
& HOVE
Blandford
Forum
Ringwood
Lyndhurst
Fareham
M27
Havant
Arundel
Wimborne
Minster
New Forest
75
A27
Chichester
6
61
Brockenhurst
Fawley
Gosport
South
Hayling
Littlehampton
Worthing
A31
Lymington
The Solent
PORTSMOUTH
Bognor
Regis
A35
Poole
73
Cowe
Ryde
Selsey
A351
Christchurch
Seaview
Selsey Bill
Wareham
BOURNEMOUTH
Yarmouth
Newport
Wool
Isle of
Purbeck
A3054
ISLE OF
WIGHT
Sandown
The Needles
A3055
Shanklin
Swanage
Durlston
Head
Ventnor
St. Catherine's
Point
CHANNEL
ISLANDS
Alderney
Guernsey
Herm
Sark
Jersey

©Maidenhead Cartographic, 2010

Map 4   25

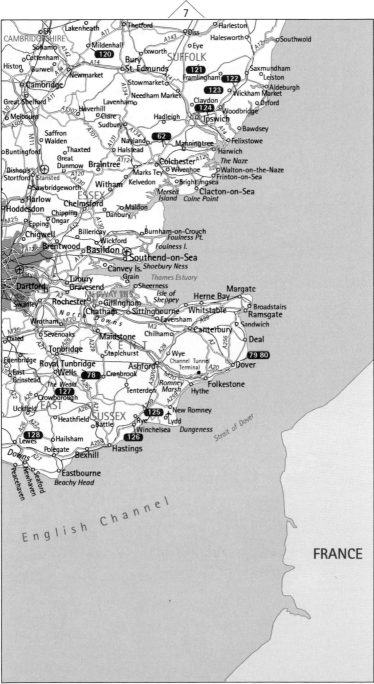

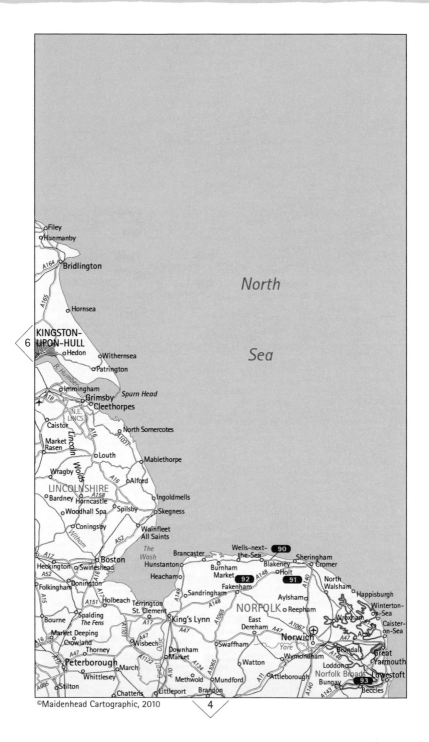

North

Sea

Filey
Hunmanby
A164 Bridlington
A165
Hornsea
KINGSTON-
UPON-HULL
6
Hedon Withernsea
R. Humber Patrington
Immingham Spurn Head
A18 Grimsby
Cleethorpes
N.E.
LNCS
Caistor
North Somercotes
A16
Market
Rasen Lincoln
Louth Mablethorpe
Wragby Wolds
A16 Alford
LINCOLNSHIRE
A158
Bardney Horncastle Ingoldmells
Woodhall Spa Spilsby Skegness
Coningsby Wainfleet
Witham All Saints
A52
The Brancaster Wells-next- 90
Wash the-Sea Sheringham
Heckington Swineshead Boston Hunstanton Blakeney Cromer
A52 Burnham Holt North
Folkingham Heacham Market 92 A148 91 A140 Walsham Happisburgh
Donington Fakenham
A15 A151 Holbeach Sandringham Aylsham Winterton-
Spalding Terrington Reepham on-Sea
Bourne The Fens St. Clement A148 NORFOLK Wroxham Caister-
Market Deeping King's Lynn East A1067 on-Sea
Crowland A47 Dereham A47 Norwich A47
Thorney Wisbech Downham Swaffham Yare Brundall Great
Peterborough Market Watton Wymondham Loddon Yarmouth
Whittlesey March Methwold Attleborough Norfolk Broads 93 Lowestoft
Stilton Mundford A11 Bungay Beccles
Chatteris Littleport Brandon A143

4

Map 4   25

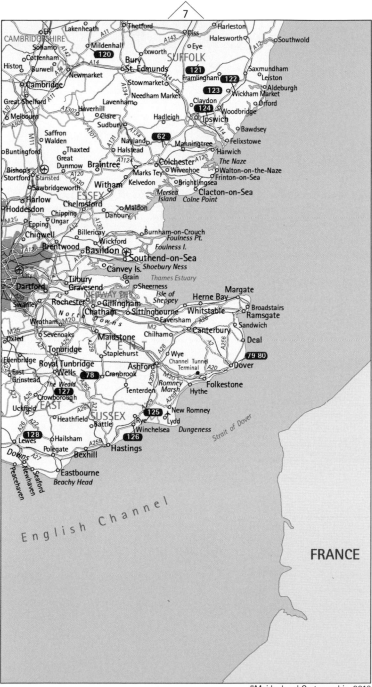

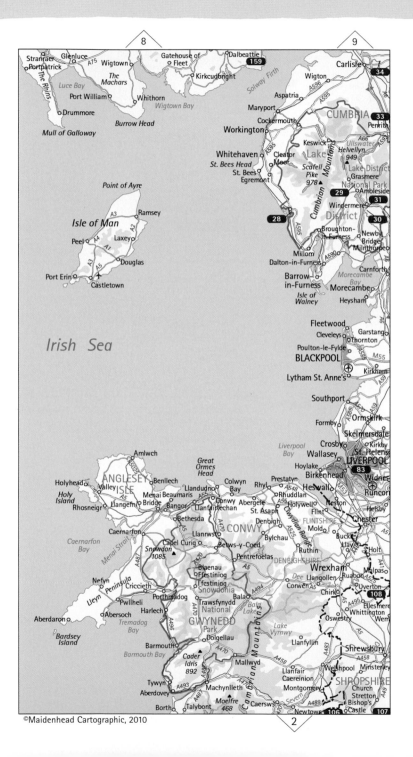

Map 6

27

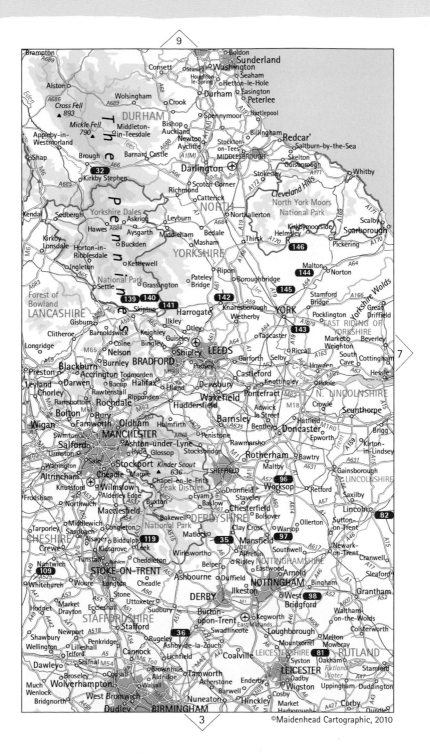

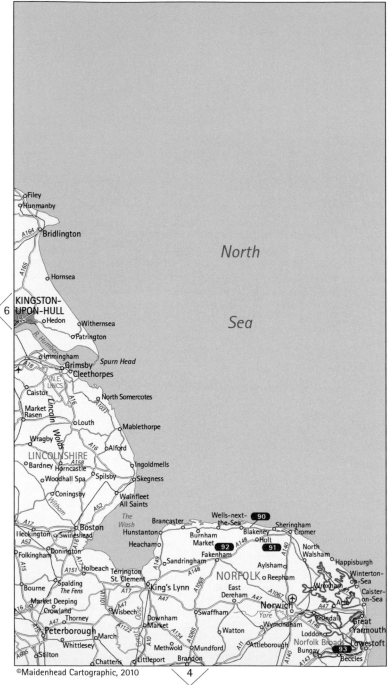

North

Sea

Filey
Hunmanby
A164 Bridlington
A165
Hornsea
KINGSTON-
UPON-HULL
6
Hedon
R. Humber
Withernsea
Patrington
Immingham
Spurn Head
A18
Grimsby
Cleethorpes
N.E.
LINCS
Caistor
A16
North Somercotes
A1031
Market
Rasen
Lincoln
Louth
Mablethorpe
Wragby
Wolds
A16
Alford
LINCOLNSHIRE
A158
Ingoldmells
Bardney
Horncastle
Woodhall Spa
Spilsby
Skegness
Coningsby
Witham
A52
Wainfleet
All Saints
A17
The
Wash
Brancaster
Wells-next-
the-Sea
90
Sheringham
Heckington
Swineshead
Boston
Hunstanton
Burnham
Blakeney
Cromer
A52
Heacham
Market
Holt
91
A140
North
Walsham
Folkingham
Donington
Fakenham
A148
Happisburgh
A15
Sandringham
A149
Sandringham
NORFOLK
Aylsham
Winterton-
on-Sea
Holbeach
Terrington
St. Clement
A148
Reepham
Wroxham
Caister-
on-Sea
Bourne
Spalding
The Fens
A17
King's Lynn
A1065
East
Dereham
A47
A1067
A47
A149
Market Deeping
A47
Wisbech
Downham
Market
Swaffham
Norwich
Yare
Brundall
Great
Yarmouth
Crowland
Thorney
Whittlesey
March
A1122
A10
A134
A1065
Watton
Wymondham
Loddon
Norfolk Broads
Lowestoft
Peterborough
Stilton
Methwold
Mundford
A11
Attleborough
A140
Bungay
93
Beccles
A605
Chatteris
Littleport
Brandon
A143

4

Map 8

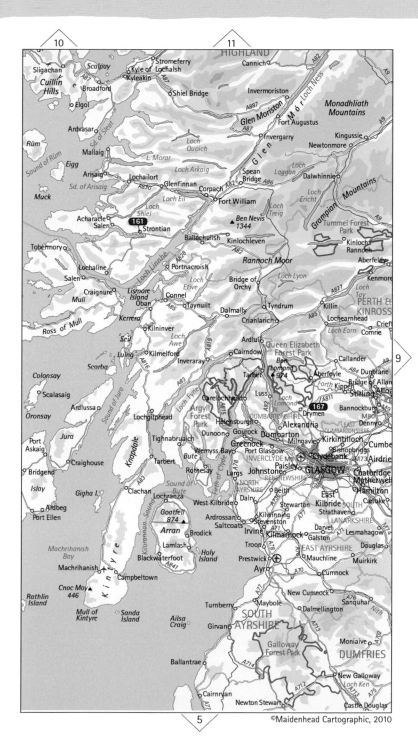

10

11

HIGHLAND

Sligachan
Scalpay
Stromeferry
Kyle of Lochalsh
Cannich
A9
Cuillin
Hills
Kyleakin
Broadford
A87
Invermoriston
Monadhliath
Mountains
Elgol
Shiel Bridge
Glen Moriston
A887
Fort Augustus
A9
Ardvasar
Sd. of Sleat
Invergarry
Kingussie
Loch
Quoich
Newtonmore
Rùm
L. Morar
Mallaig
Glen
Loch Arkaig
Spean
Bridge
Loch
Laggan
Dalwhinnie
Eigg
Arisaig
Lochailort
A830
Glenfinnan
Corpach
A82
A86
Muck
Sd. of Arisaig
Loch Eil
Fort William
Loch
Ericht
Grampian
Mountains
Acharacle
Salen
161
Strontian
Loch
Shiel
Ben Nevis
1344
Loch
Treig
Tummel Forest
Park
A9
Tobermory
Ballachulish
Kinlochleven
Kinloch
Rannoch
Lochaline
Portnacroish
Rannoch Moor
A82
Aberfeldy
Salen
Loch
Etive
Bridge of
Orchy
Loch Lyon
Kenmore
Craignure
Lismore
Island
Connel
A828
Loch Linnhe
Loch
Tay
PERTH &
KINROSS
Mull
Oban
Kerrera
A85
Taynuilt
Dalmally
Tyndrum
Killin
Lochearnhead
Crief
Ross of Mull
Kilninver
Crianlarich
A85
Comrie
Loch
Awe
A819
Ardlui
Loch Earn
Scil
Cairndow
Queen Elizabeth
Forest Park
9
Luing
Kilmelford
A816
Inveraray
Ben
Lomond
974
Callander
A84
Dunblane
Scarba
A83
Tarbet
Aberfoyle
Bridge of Allan
Colonsay
Garelochhead
Luss
Loch
Lomond
A811
Kippen
Stirling
Alloa
Scalasaig
Argyll
Forest
Park
A82
Forth
Drymen
167
Bannockburn
Oronsay
Ardlussa
Lochgilphead
Helensburgh
DUMBARTONSHIRE
Denny
M80
A9
Jura
Tighnabruaich
Dunoon
Gourock
Dumbarton
EAST
Milngavie
Kirkintilloch
Cumbe
Port
Askaig
Knapdale
Tarbert
A83
Wemyss Bay
Bute
Port Glasgow
Greenock
Paisley
INVERCLYDE
RENFREWSHIRE
Bishopbriggs
Clydebank
A73
Airdrie
Coatbridge
Bridgend
Craighouse
Rothesay
Largs
Johnstone
GLASGOW
Motherwel
Islay
Gigha I.
Clachan
Sound of
Bute
NORTH
AYRSHIRE
Beith
East
Kilbride
SOUTH
Hamilton
Carluke
Ardbeg
Port Ellen
Lochranza
West Kilbride
Dalry
Stewarton
Strathaven
LANARKSHIRE
Darvel
Lesmahagow
Goatfell
874
Arran
Brodick
Kilwinning
Ardrossan
Stevenston
Saltcoats
Irvine
Kilmarnock
A71
Galston
Douglas
EAST AYRSHIRE
Muirkirk
Lamlash
Holy
Island
A841
Troon
A78
Mauchline
Machrihanish
Bay
Blackwaterfoot
Prestwick
Ayr
A70
Cumnock
Machrihanish
Campbeltown
A77
New Cumnock
Sanquhar
A76
Cnoc Moy
446
Maybole
Turnberry
SOUTH
AYRSHIRE
Dalmellington
Moniaive
A702
Rathlin
Island
Mull of
Kintyre
Sanda
Island
Ailsa
Craig
Girvan
Galloway
Forest Park
DUMFRIES
A713
Ballantrae
A714
New Galloway
A712
Loch Ken
Cairnryan
A77
Newton Stewart
Castle Douglas

5

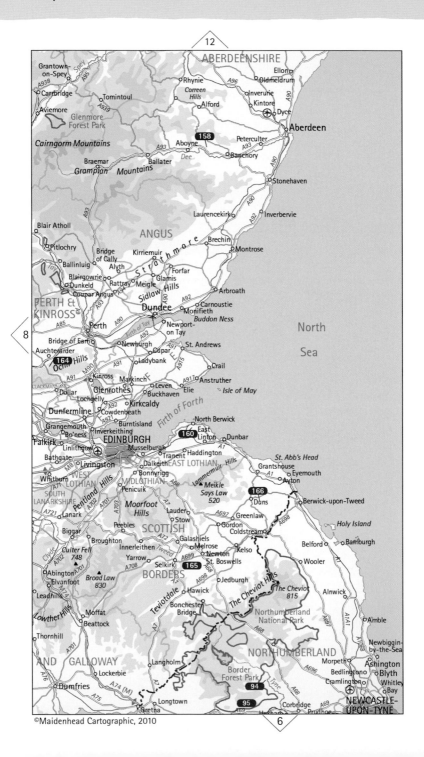

Map 10

31

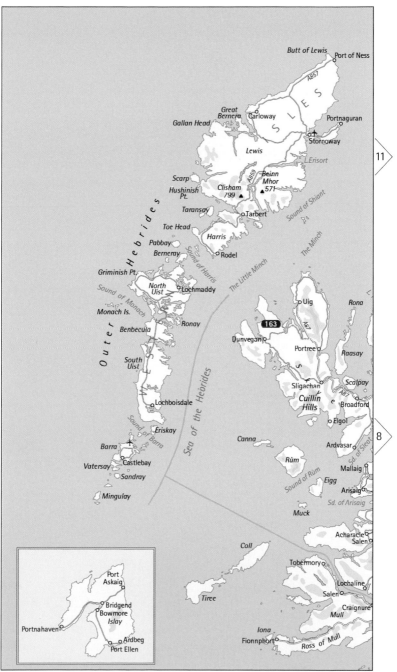

©Maidenhead Cartographic, 2010

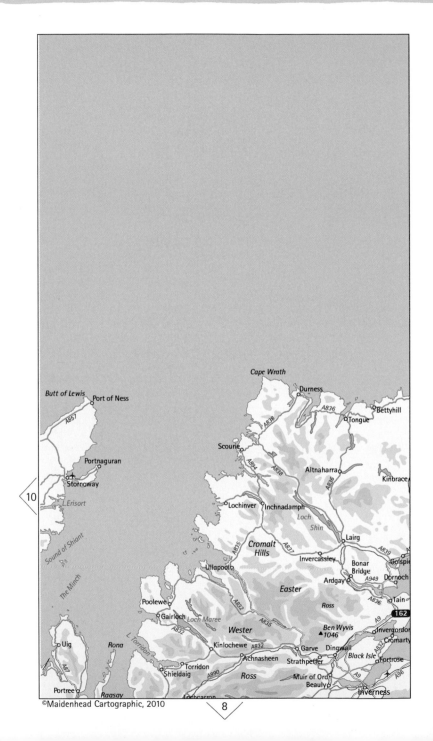

Map 12   33

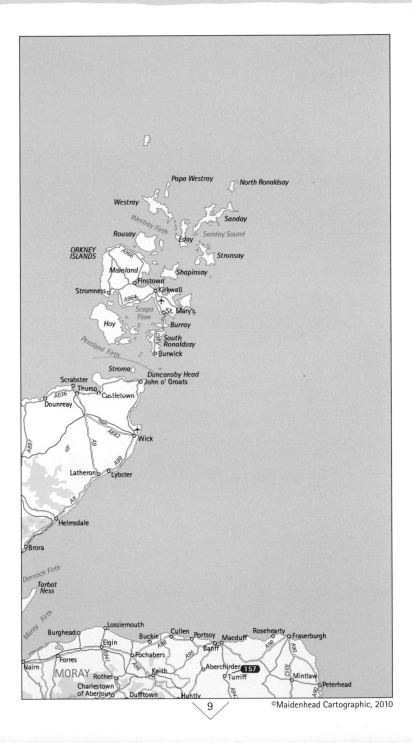

©Maidenhead Cartographic, 2010

England

Bathwick Gardens

The hand-printed period wallpaper is just one of the remarkable features of this elegant Grade I-listed house, in one of Bath's finest Regency terraces five minutes walk from the centre. It has been so authentically restored that the BBC used its rooms for Jane Austen's *Persuasion*. If you're looking for a spacious yet graceful city venue for a meeting or a special birthday party, Mechthild and Julian's lavish house is a perfect choice. The lovely dining and drawing rooms can combine to take up to 60 guests, the library provides a break-out space and the catering – including themed Regency meals – can be arranged seamlessly. Big light bedrooms have a sleigh bed or stunning views; one stylish bathroom combines marquina marble, cherrywood and ebony. Parties over eight wishing to stay can spill over into the charming, cosy coach house at the end of the garden. Have breakfast in the family kitchen, the conservatory or out in the garden. Mechthild can serve up an Austrian alternative of cold meats and cheeses, fresh rye breads and homemade cakes, and she loves guests to practise their German with her. Herrlich!

Room hire	3: Board (max 20). Cabaret (max 40). Reception (max 60).
Catering	In-house, approved & own caterers.
Sleeps	8 B&B.
Closed	Rarely.
Directions	A46 to Bath, then A4 for city centre. Left onto A36 over Cleveland Bridge; follow signs to Holburne Museum. Directly after museum, left. House on right.

Mechthild Self von Hippel
95 Sydney Place, Bath BA2 6NE
Tel   +44 (0)1225 469435
Email   visitus@bathwickgardens.co.uk
Web   www.bathwickgardens.co.uk

Laurel Farm

Tucked in the Somerset hills lies a small reverie of orchards, sheep, pigs, poultry, and spring-fed ponds buzzing with wildlife. At its heart stands a little former Buddhist stone and glass temple, from whose roof a bronze Buddha gazes serenely over the Mendips. As well as planting over 900 trees since his arrival at Laurel Farm, Ross has revamped the open-plan building into a light natural space that can become just about whatever you want. Adjustable tables and AV facilities appear for meetings; retreats and yoga classes have floor cushions; for parties, let your inner designer go wild (or just ask for the ten-foot cinema screen). For self-caterers, a well-equipped kitchen does the trick; a nearby company can also provide delicious locally sourced meals. Warm, dynamic and exuding straightforward Irish charm, Ross can facilitate workshops or lead team-building activities in the six-acre grounds. He's even found time to build a sweet eco-friendly cottage! Ten miles from Bath in the midst of peace and nature, this is a place to reflect, reconnect, contemplate, meditate, or just think and breathe more deeply.

Room hire	1: Board (max 18). Cabaret (max 24). Theatre (max 24). Reception (max 25).
Catering	Approved & own caterers.
Sleeps	5 S/C.
Closed	Rarely.
Directions	A367 Bath to Radstock. Take Peasedown St. John turning, down Keels Hill (opp. Catholic Church). Entrance left after 0.75 miles beside Carlingcott sign.

Ethical Collection: Community.
See page 208 for details

Ross Thompson
17 Carlingcott,
Peasedown St. John, Bath BA2 8AN

Tel	+44 (0)1761 420204
Email	ross@laurelfarm.org.uk
Web	www.laurelfarm.org.uk

The Elephant at Pangbourne

Elephants everywhere – all benign, including those in the Ba-bar. This is a super hotel on the edge of town, renovated in unremitting style and perfect for smaller wedding receptions, with the pretty church a two-minute walk. Great for celebrations of every kind, and meetings too. Whatever the occasion, let the super-competent team take care of your every wish; the chef can whip up a full wedding breakfast or a delicious buffet and the menu is yours to create. Dance the night away in the opulent and lavish Elephant Room, all regal colours and beautiful Indian furniture. Bridal couples can choose from an array of delightfully eclectic bedrooms that spin you round the world in style, and there's heaps of room for family and friends. The colonial style Nelly Room, with natural light streaming in, is perfect for a small meeting; enjoy a simple 'tiffin' for your working lunch, or a sumptuous meal in the restaurant. Walk it off with a stroll along the Thames, perhaps a spot of golf or horse riding. And if this feels too much like hard work then join the locals and sink into huge sofas in front of the fire.

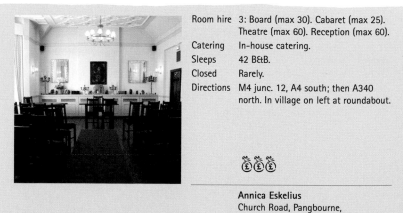

Room hire	3: Board (max 30). Cabaret (max 25). Theatre (max 60). Reception (max 60).
Catering	In-house catering.
Sleeps	42 B&B.
Closed	Rarely.
Directions	M4 junc. 12, A4 south; then A340 north. In village on left at roundabout.

Annica Eskelius
Church Road, Pangbourne,
Reading RG8 7AR

Tel	+44 (0)1189 842244
Email	reception@elephanthotel.co.uk
Web	www.elephanthotel.co.uk

Queen's Eyot

Boating cross river to a private island for the day would normally be wishful thinking. Not so on Queen's Eyot: four acres steeped in Eton College rowing history cause the Thames to fork and make way for this exclusive setting. Lovely for a party or corporate gathering, it's at its most magical for weddings. Parties often glide upstream from Windsor before disembarking onto the wharf between the trees bathing their leaves in the waters. Once inside the clubhouse, a suspended single-scull greets you from among a higgledy-piggledy mass of scrubbed beams. From here, step through French windows and hanging baskets to the lawn, ringed by cherry damsons and walnut trees; it stretches and widens to allow for croquet and jazz bands, then tapers to a lovely secluded arbour. The main stages for conferences, wedding breakfasts and celebratory meals are the versatile clubroom and a marquee that can be dressed up to the nines, but whether it's hog roast or haute cuisine you're after, depend upon Malcolm and Ruth, the husband and wife stewards of the island, to come up with the best. *No civil licence.*

Room hire	1 + marquee: Board (max 20). Cabaret (max 150). Theatre (max 150). Reception (max 200).
Catering	In-house catering.
Closed	November to March.
Directions	From Windsor A308 signed Maidenhead, past Oakley Court hotel, right into Monkey Island Lane signed Bray Marina, entrance to Queen's Eyot Club on right.

£ £ £ £

Angela Leslie
Monkey Island Lane, Bray SL6 2EA

Tel	+44 (0)1753 832756
Email	info@queenseyot.co.uk
Web	www.queenseyot.co.uk

Woodbrooke Quaker Study Centre

Such a pleasure to find a vast, green, tranquil space so close to Birmingham city centre. A pleasure, too, to be welcomed by people dedicated to protecting its variety of trees, its running water, its lake inhabited by kingfishers and heron, its Victorian walled garden. The gleaming white Georgian-style mansion, with a beautifully tiled entrance hall and an Edwardian extension, was donated to the Quakers by George Cadbury as a place of study and meeting and has seven function rooms for gatherings large and small. The Cadbury Room is well-equipped and has lovely garden views, while the light-bathed Quiet Room is perfect for prayer, a private ceremony or a more contemplative meeting. A library, art room and lounge are also available for guests. Stroll to the dining room for fresh buffet-style meals – they can cater for special dietary needs too; a wedding party could use the lawn for (non-alcoholic) drinks. There are bedrooms galore, including many singles; residential courses and longer meetings are well catered for. Staff exude warmth and enthusiasm and the entire experience is one of serenity and peace. *No alcohol.*

Ethical Collection: Environment; Community; Food. See page 208 for details

Room hire	7: Board (max 35). Cabaret (max 45). Theatre (max 100). Reception (max 100).
Catering	In-house catering.
Sleeps	65 B&B.
Closed	Christmas & Boxing Day.
Directions	Buses from Birmingham city centre and Selly Oak train station. On A38 Bristol Rd, four miles south of Birmingham city.

Kirstie McAra
1046 Bristol Road,
Birmingham B29 6LJ
Tel   +44 (0)121 472 5171
Email   conferences@woodbrooke.org.uk
Web   www.woodbrooke.org.uk

Drakes

If you were to compile a list of chic city-wedding retreats, Drakes would surely be on it. A shame to miss out on one moment of this fabulous hotel's exemplary service, superb food, decadent vibe and groovy design; come for the whole weekend. Gather a handful of your loved ones, take over the hotel and celebrate, or marry, in a reception room that is intimate, funky and sophisticated all at the same time. Pose on the flower-decked staircase, then shimmy off to the beach below for champagne; or spread your picnic blankets on the pebbles and enjoy canapés. Your three-course wedding breakfast (no buffets) is a fabulous take on modern European food, served in a stylish restaurant. The bedrooms are wonderful and bridal couples are utterly spoilt in a heavenly room with a seven-foot-wide bed, floor-to-ceiling windows and a freestanding bath; gaze out to sea as you soak. Old and new meet in this listed building equipped with WiFi throughout; and business meetings and presentations can be followed by a sailing trip that takes off pretty much from the door. Laid-back glamour at its best.

Room hire	3: Board (max 12). Cabaret (max 25). Theatre (max 18). Reception (max 40).
Catering	In-house catering.
Sleeps	40 B&B.
Closed	Never.
Directions	M23 & A23 into Brighton. At seafront, with pier in front, turn left up the hill. Drakes on left after 300 yds.

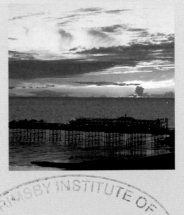

Richard Hayes
43-44 Marine Parade,
Brighton BN2 1PE

Tel	+44 (0)1273 696934
Email	info@drakesofbrighton.com
Web	www.drakesofbrighton.com

Bristol

Brunel's ss Great Britain

Sweep through the gates of the Great Western Dockyard – or pull up by water taxi – to step aboard the world's first luxury liner. Designed by Brunel in 1843, fully restored to her former glory, she basks alongside Bristol's bustling waterway with flags a-flutter; it would be difficult to find a more striking setting for a wedding, meeting or party. Glide down the aisle of the Promenade Deck, sweet with the scent of fresh flowers, and marry under the huge skylight. Children will delight in exploring the on-board museum while you mingle on the upper deck, drink in hand, surrounded by an expanse of sparkling water. As night falls, city lights twinkle across the water and the ship glows in her glass 'sea'. Dine in style in the plush First-Class Saloon, all red carpets, columns and gold leaf. The Hayward Saloon is great for meetings and private dinners, and has its own cocktail bar; for larger business events, head next door to the brand-new Lecture Theatre. Charming, efficient Bronwen (ever on hand, with tissues and safety pins) and jolly Captain Bob keep it all shipshape and Bristol fashion.

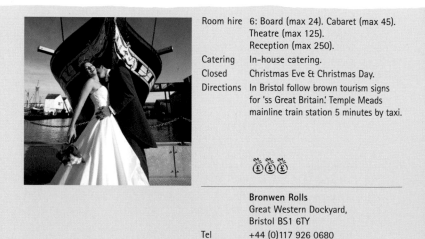

Room hire	6: Board (max 24). Cabaret (max 45). Theatre (max 125). Reception (max 250).
Catering	In-house catering.
Closed	Christmas Eve & Christmas Day.
Directions	In Bristol follow brown tourism signs for 'ss Great Britain'. Temple Meads mainline train station 5 minutes by taxi.

Bronwen Rolls
Great Western Dockyard,
Bristol BS1 6TY

Tel	+44 (0)117 926 0680
Email	events@ssgreatbritain.org
Web	www.ssgreatbritain.org

Bordeaux Quay

Come for the food! Bordeaux Quay sets the standard in sustainable catering, winning awards for its delicious delivery of seasonal, local and organic produce. The imposing glass-fronted building gleams on Bristol's riverside, renovated to high eco standards and converted from wine warehouse to (take a deep breath) restaurant, bar, brasserie, deli, bakery and cookery school. The bar and brasserie are on the ground floor: smart, swish and flooded with natural light. Up a flight of pale oak stairs is the restaurant, a glamorous space of aubergine and cream hues, original industrial pillars and an open kitchen in which the chefs star. It is the perfect venue for wedding receptions, launches or celebrations: they'll arrange flowers, canapés or a multi-course meal, a spectacular wedding cake, a dance floor; there's even space for a jazz band. Smaller parties or meetings can have a private dining room, and take tailormade cookery courses or cocktail master classes in the wine bar. If great food, good service and high ethical standards matter, this is the place for you. *No civil licence.*

Room hire	3: Board (max 20). Cabaret (max 110). Theatre (max 70). Reception (max 140).
Catering	In-house catering. Locally sourced & organic.
Closed	Rarely.
Directions	Bristol city centre, on waterfront, directions on website. Easy access by car, foot, train, bus and ferry.

Sarah Jones
V Shed, Cannons Way,
Bristol BS1 5UH

Tel	+44 (0)117 906 5552
Email	info@bordeaux-quay.co.uk
Web	www.bordeaux-quay.co.uk

St George's Bristol

Hard to believe you're in bustling Bristol – this graceful Greek Revival 19th-century church, all columns and cupola in tranquil grounds, is now an internationally renowned concert hall and a fine setting for wedding receptions, parties and corporate gatherings. The jewel in St George's crown is its huge auditorium – an elegant room with sprung wooden floors, double height windows and a ceiling dominated by grand chandeliers. You get excellent views of the stage and gilded reredos from the gallery; backstage, purple velvet sofas await flagging brides or nervous speakers. Ask bubbly event manager Jenny about approved local suppliers for corporate dinners and wedding breakfasts. Party downstairs in the Crypt, with its licensed bar, flagged floors, stone walls and mood lighting; for meetings choose the smaller Doric Room, or RTZ room (a soundproof recording studio). There's room for three marquees among benches and trees in the split-level gardens; a long flight of stone steps to the striking classical façade for a dramatic photo backdrop; and, impressively, disabled access throughout. *No civil licence.*

Ethical Collection: Food.
See page 208 for details

Room hire	4 + marquee: Board (max 40). Cabaret (max 750). Theatre (max 562). Reception (max 750).
Catering	Approved caterers.
Closed	Rarely.
Directions	From Bristol city centre head towards College Green on A4, up Park Street then left onto Great George Street.

Jenny Hutchinson
Great George Street, Bristol BS1 5RR

Tel	+44 (0)117 929 4929
Email	j.hutchinson@stgeorgesbristol.co.uk
Web	www.stgeorgesbristol.co.uk

Glassboat

Swans glide by, rowing boats zip along, boats chug past – moored in the centre of Bristol, the Glassboat's river view is cinematic. From its 1920s role as timber barge, the boat has been transformed into a restaurant, bar and party venue with a stunning meld of floor-to-ceiling glass and architectural salvage: check out polished walnut floors from Courage's Brewery, a marble bar from St Nicholas's fish market, portholes from a cross-channel ferry. Step aboard to the cosy lounge bar, lined with gleaming glasses and spirits; to your right is a smart, sleek restaurant whose glass aft section allows wonderful river views. Sunny by day, it becomes twinkly and gorgeous at night. For a private dinner or meeting, the cosy lower deck seats 40 amid purple walls pierced by portholes; if music is your thing, this space can hold a DJ and small dance floor as well. With charming staff and an excellent choice of fresh Mediterranean 'sunshine food', it's great for anniversaries, birthdays, receptions, meetings, launches and networking events – all served with ever-changing views and a generous sprinkling of style.

Room hire	3: Board (max 30). Cabaret (max 140). Theatre (max 40). Reception (max 200).
Catering	In-house catering.
Closed	Never.
Directions	Central Bristol, directions on website. 10 minute walk or ferry ride from Bristol Temple Meads railway station. 10 minute walk from coach station.

Arne Ringner
Welsh Back, Bristol BS1 4SB

Tel	+44 (0)117 929 0704
Email	restaurant@glassboat.co.uk
Web	www.glassboat.co.uk

Circomedia

Drama: this former church has it in sparkling hatfuls, from the tiered Gothic tower (nicknamed 'the wedding cake') to the aerial rig for high-flying entertainments. Rescued by Lottery money, the 18th-century Church of St Paul now nurtures a circus arts school. Rising from leafy Portland Square it is encircled by Georgian townhouses with wrought-iron gates, old-fashioned street lamps, a traditional red phone box. City central, in vibrant and edgy St. Paul's, the square itself is quiet. Inside, the main space soars up to an original ornate stucco ceiling; sunshine floods through stained glass; at night, stone columns are majestically uplit. Round tables leave a central arena for dancing or performers; wooden pews line up for theatre seating. Hire an aerialist, jugglers, magician (or a DJ for the excellent PA system). Smaller gatherings can take a welcoming aperitif in the next-door glass-walled gallery. Jo will help with your event plans. For business, there's a small boardroom – or try stretching team-building exercises with tightwire, stiltwalking, trapeze. *Consecrated church for religious weddings.*

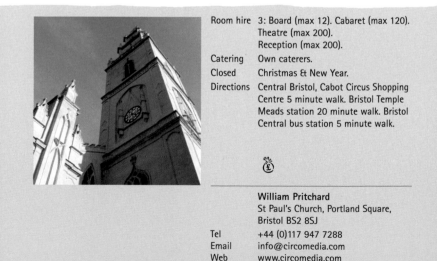

Room hire	3: Board (max 12). Cabaret (max 120). Theatre (max 200). Reception (max 200).
Catering	Own caterers.
Closed	Christmas & New Year.
Directions	Central Bristol, Cabot Circus Shopping Centre 5 minute walk. Bristol Temple Meads station 20 minute walk. Bristol Central bus station 5 minute walk.

William Pritchard
St Paul's Church, Portland Square,
Bristol BS2 8SJ

Tel	+44 (0)117 947 7288
Email	info@circomedia.com
Web	www.circomedia.com

Lido Bristol

Kick off your shoes and strip off suits and ties: Bristol's Lido is a brilliant venue for any event whose aim is good old-fashioned fun. People have whooped it up here since Victorian times but facilities are now superbly 21st-century, combining high ecological standards with a nod to nostalgia and a touch of flair. A solar-heated outdoor pool is framed by foliage and stripy curtained cubicles; a hot tub steams gently, and inside is a luxury spa with sauna, steam and massage rooms. For an informal meeting with good coffee and cakes, the glass-walled café bar along one side of the pool is perfect, especially at night when the water glimmers with light. Larger events take place in the upstairs restaurant, also glass-walled and overlooking the pool; fabulous food with a Middle Eastern tinge emerges like magic from the open kitchen and wood-fired oven. True to its roots, the Lido's popular with the public, but you can also hire the place exclusively for two delicious hours. Quirky, cool and reliably well-managed – a fun and stylish space for a small event. *No civil licence.*

Room hire	2: Cabaret (max 90). Reception (max 200).
Catering	In-house catering.
Closed	Never.
Directions	From Bristol city centre, turn left off Whiteladies Road onto St Paul's Road, then first right.

Arne Ringner
Oakfield Place, Clifton,
Bristol BS8 2BJ

Tel	+44 (0)117 933 9530
Email	spa@lidobristol.com
Web	www.lidobristol.com

The Pierian Centre

Community, spirituality, creativity and cultural awareness lie at the heart of this intimate centre, which welcomes events of all sizes. The Grade I-listed Georgian townhouse, set in a city-centre square, spreads itself over five storeys, from a deep well to a stunning domed skylight. The Freeman Room dresses up beautifully in banquet cloths and fresh flowers, while extraordinary twisted wooden sculptures stand guard; the smaller Music Room (with piano) hosts concerts, rehearsals or courses. The sunny Lounge Room's sofas invite informal meetings and counselling sessions; the Healing Room's calming yellows make it perfect for one-to-ones. At mealtimes head to the Morning Room or Old Kitchen: a local Caribbean chef works closely with the centre or you can choose from a list of caterers. It's an intimate venue for a wedding, and, if your guest list tops 50, you can arrange to parade across to Circomedia for the reception; perhaps to enjoy an aerial display. Dynamic and accommodating, June and her team are focused on the centre's social purpose – a space that is both chilled-out and inspiring.

Ethical Collection: Community.
See page 208 for details

Room hire	6: Board (max 30). Cabaret (max 50). Theatre (max 60). Reception (max 80).
Catering	Approved & own caterers.
Closed	Mondays.
Directions	In Bristol city centre, off M32. See website for details.

June Burrough
27 Portland Square, St. Paul's, Bristol BS2 8SA

Tel	+44 (0)117 924 4512
Email	info@pieriancentre.com
Web	www.pierian-centre.com

Paintworks Event Space

The Paintworks Event Space is seriously funky, from the feel of the place to the friendly staff. Your guests will feel cool as they wend their way to this former paint factory, set in what was an industrial wasteland, now a canal-side working village and home to all sorts of media and artistic ventures. It's a vast, blank, thrillingly flexible canvas for you to let your creativity go wild. Basic ingredients include a structure of huge steel columns, rough and ready red-brick walls, high windows sucking in natural light (the roof girders hold spotlights too), half-wood, half-concrete floors, a mezzanine gallery, break-out spaces, a curtain and panels to tweak the room's size and shape... Launch parties, exhibitions, charity events, gigs, performances, fairs, award ceremonies, weddings, meetings, film and photo shoots, all work fantastically in this off-beat yet trendy, even glamorous space. Guests spill out to one of two courtyards (small or large), decorated with arty murals; in-house caterers and helpful staff can handle events of any size. Young and fresh, Paintworks is a wow of a place!

Room hire	1: Board (max 30). Cabaret (max 250). Theatre (max 300). Reception (max 500).
Catering	In-house, approved & own caterers.
Closed	Christmas Day.
Directions	From central Bristol follow sign for Temple Meads Railway Station, continue along A4 (Bath Road) for 0.5 miles. Paintworks on left.

Natalie Franco
Main Courtyard, Paintworks, Bath Road
Bristol BS4 3EH

Tel	+44 (0)117 971 4320
Email	natalie@paintworksbristol.co.uk
Web	www.paintworksevents.co.uk

Weddings • Parties • Meetings

Wooda Farm

Shelved into the sunny slope of a dramatic hideaway valley, wrapped in bluebell woods, semi-wild: a home for inspired gatherings and artistic escapades. The high-beamed barn – picture windows, rough stone walls, smooth plaster – can host wedding receptions, rehearsals, presentations; the mostly double-height space neatly transforms into an auditorium with audio-visual gizmos, its mezzanine converting into curved seating platforms. There's a glass-walled studio retreat too, where views reach over fields criss-crossed by ancient hedges, and visitors can lodge in the cottage. Or (if you're booking the venue) as guests in Max and Gary's easy-going old farmhouse. Deeply involved in developing their Soil Association certified organic farm, Max has a background in theatre and Gary is chief caterer; both are likeable, professional, human. A vegetarian himself but a cook for all, Gary is a fan of Slow Food, foraging, their terraced veg plot – and the Wooda hens. The farm has a wind turbine and its own spring, sheep, a horse, and a mule. Twenty acres of roaming and the coast two miles away – wonderful. *No civil licence.*

Ethical Collection: Environment; Community; Food. See page 208 for details

Room hire	2: Board (max 30). Cabaret (max 50). Theatre (max 50). Reception (max 100).
Catering	In-house catering. Locally sourced & organic.
Sleeps	12: 8 DB&B; 4 S/C.
Closed	Never.
Directions	A39 towards Bude or Camelford . B3263 to Boscastle, right after 1 mile to Crackington H. After Hentervene, track to Wooda 250 yds on right.

Max Burrows & Gary Whitbread
Crackington Haven, Bude EX23 0LF

Tel   +44 (0)1840 230129
Email   max@woodafarm.co.uk
Web   www.woodafarm.co.uk

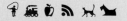

Upton Farm

Scrunch up a swathe of white granite to Upton Farm, high above the sea with panoramic sea views. The owners have transformed the farm outbuildings into three exceptionally comfortable holiday homes and the whole place works beautifully as an informal party or wedding venue. The Long Room is a simple, pretty, whitewashed stone barn with wooden rafters and you can decorate it as you wish – excellent for a wedding party of up to 50. (And there's an award-winning florists down the road if you want help with the greenery!). Spill out of French doors into the courtyard for drinks and sparkling sea views. Caterers can be organised, local and organic food is encouraged, wine is from a local supplier – or you can bring your own; in summer you can barbecue on the lawn and dance the night away. Bedrooms in the cottages are light, fresh, pristine and on the ground floor. Find all you need for a family get-together, a shooting party or an awayday: generous sofas and a wood-burner, coir carpets strewn with rugs, shelves stocked with good books and games, high-spec kitchens with big tables. Lovely.

Room hire	2: Cabaret (max 50). Theatre (max 50), Reception (max 50).
Catering	Approved caterers. Locally sourced & organic.
Sleeps	25: 6 B&B; 19 S/C.
Closed	Rarely.
Directions	South thro' Delabole, right into Treligga Downs Rd; right at T-junc. towards Trebarwith; Farm on right after 1 mile.

Elizabeth & Ricardo Dorich
Trebarwith PL33 9DG

Tel	+44 (0)1840 770225
Email	ricardo.dorich@homecall.co.uk
Web	www.upton-farm.co.uk

The Mill House Inn

Coast down a steep winding lane to the 1760s mill house in a peaceful woodland spot, with Trebarwith's spectacular sandy beach a ten-minute walk away. What a setting for a relaxed and laid-back wedding! You will be happy as a Cornish clam here whatever your jamboree: come for informal birthday parties, weddings or meetings and you will be charmed. Mark and Kep are happy to be with you every step of the way – they'll organise a marquee for numbers over 120, flowers, band, barn dance, a hog or duck roast by the burbling stream; there's even a duck race! Inside: log fires, a fine flagged floor, wooden tables, leather sofas and a swanky dining room with views over the stream; it's light, elegant, very modern and the chef serves delicious and innovative food – much of it Cornish including halibut almost straight from the sea. Bedrooms are all different: simple and uncluttered with a contemporary feel, smaller rooms with neat showers – and a sprinkling of red rose petals on the bed and bath for honeymooners. Walking, biking, surfing, crabbing... and perfect photo opportunities on the beach.

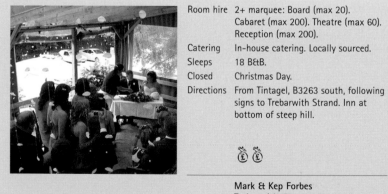

Room hire	2+ marquee: Board (max 20). Cabaret (max 200). Theatre (max 60). Reception (max 200).
Catering	In-house catering. Locally sourced.
Sleeps	18 B&B.
Closed	Christmas Day.
Directions	From Tintagel, B3263 south, following signs to Trebarwith Strand. Inn at bottom of steep hill.

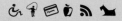

Mark & Kep Forbes
Trebarwith, Tintagel PL34 0HD

Tel	+44 (0)1840 770200
Email	management@themillhouseinn.co.uk
Web	www.themillhouseinn.co.uk

Cornish Tipi Holidays

Bright tipis glimmer in a secret wooded glade; a path wends down to a trout-filled swimming lake – a unique and special setting for a celebration, reunion or retreat. Weddings take place in a licensed new pavilion down by the tinkling stream. Caterers, brewers, photographers, puppeteers, storytellers swoop in; Cornish pipers or Celtic harps strike up; then rollick into the night with a ceilidh. Fairy lights sparkle your way back, the only other light from moon and stars. Each canvas tipi reaches 18 feet high, a light, spacious cocoon supported by hessian-bound poles and bright with oriental rugs, lanterns, hand-painted covers. Pick your spot privately, side-by-side or in a cluster. Nature romps gloriously around you: cooking is over an open fire, electricity comes from sun and wind. Showers and loos are shared. Elizabeth's family have lived near this old quarry for generations and we've recommended her tipi holidays for years (adults love it – children even more). Wildlife abounds, the trout are excellent; lake, stream and Cornish coast are all nearby and outdoor and team-building activities are easily arranged.

Room hire	Wedding pavilion, tipi, marquee: Board (max 25). Cabaret (max 300). Theatre (max 25). Reception (max 300).
Catering	Approved & own caterers.
Sleeps	200 S/C.
Closed	November to March.
Directions	From A395, follow B3314 to and through Delabole; left at Port Gaverne crossroads, 1.5 miles.

Elizabeth Tom
Tregeare, Pendoggett, St Kew PL30 3LW
Tel   +44 (0)1208 880781
Email   info@cornishtipiholidays.co.uk
Web   www.cornishtipiholidays.co.uk

Headland Hotel

Sunlight streams through huge windows, almost blinding you to the panorama of Atlantic waves crashing over Britain's surfing mecca. The striking red-brick Victorian hotel blends in beautifully with the AONB headland around it. A glorious exception to the rule that large hotels aren't intimate or flexible, this one allows you three or 300 guests at your wedding – and you can marry in whatever you like, from surf gear to top hat and tails. Hold a breakfast meeting or a banquet, a small workshop or a big conference. Hit the surf for team-building days; throw a cocktail party in the zingy bar. And, when the evening's over, float up the grand staircase (handy for photo shoots) to stylish bedrooms; you can stay in super-smart cottages, too. Newly-weds should book the sumptuous Bridal Suite, a fantasy of dove greys, sea greens and teal silk. Everything's here – tennis courts, pools, spa, golf course, croquet lawn, even a sprung dance floor inside. Come for genuinely friendly staff, concern for the environment, delicious food, and the raw beauty of the Cornish coast. Fistral Beach and the Headland Hotel are fabulous.

Room hire	8: Board (max 30). Cabaret (max 300). Theatre (max 200). Reception (max 300).
Catering	In-house catering. Locally sourced.
Sleeps	266: 104 B&B; 1 S/C apartment; 39 S/C cottages.
Closed	Christmas Eve, Day & Boxing Day.
Directions	A392 to Newquay, over 2 r'bouts. Take A3058, follow signs to Fistral Beach, 2nd exit at Red Lion, left onto Headland Rd. At end of road on right.

Carolyn Armstrong
Headland Road, Newquay TR7 1EW

Tel	+44 (0)1637 872211
Email	reception@headlandhotel.co.uk
Web	www.headlandhotel.co.uk

Scorrier House

The undiluted elegance of Scorrier House is clear the minute you arrive: a winding drive through a swathe of parkland leads to the door, with a large, monkey-puzzled arboretum providing the backdrop. Jaws drop further as you move inside; an Adam-designed ceiling, gilded mirrors and noble portraits of Williamses past adding to the understated decadence. Brides can make their entrance at the top of the sweeping double staircase in the Grand Hall, then sashay from room to room across polished wooden floors. Huge windows pull in the light and the views across the estate, while the drawing room flows into the conservatory, patio and gazebo beyond, leaving a wealth of choices for the ceremony itself. All is refined and gracious, a primed canvas for personal flourishes, while kind owners Richard and Caroline have all the events' experience you could need. Professional kitchens await chosen caterers, and there are smart self-catering cottages for the wedding party, too. The position couldn't be better, the grounds are a photographer's dream, and newly-weds can escape to the Cornish coast after a very special breakfast.

Room hire	2: Board (max 30). Cabaret (max 120). Theatre (max 140). Reception (max 160).
Catering	Approved & self-catering.
Sleeps	14 S/C.
Closed	Rarely.
Directions	A30, then A3047 to Scorrier. On for 0.5 miles to mini roundabout; left. Large drive on right (about 200 yds); signed.

Richard & Caroline Williams
Scorrier, Redruth TR16 5AU
Tel   +44 (0)1209 820264
Email   rwill10442@aol.com
Web   www.scorrierhouse.co.uk

Trerose Manor

Follow winding lanes through glorious countryside to find an extremely pretty listed manor house with a beamed reception hall and a warm family atmosphere. The reception hall is oak-floored with a stone fireplace, the drawing room is elegant and beautiful, the library is cedar panelled, candlelit and warmed by a stove – and the church is five minutes up the lane. You can spill out to the terrace for drinks and food; it's picture perfect for parties and small weddings. (The clock tower is lit up at night and there are plenty of wedding photo options.) Tessa loves to look after you and will cook a sumptuous and locally sourced feast for groups of 25 and more; she can also advise on local caterers for bigger bashes. Two large, light bedrooms sit peacefully in your own wing and have views over the stunning garden. Each is dressed in pretty colours, has comfy seats and smart bathrooms; the French Room with a chaise longue is a honey of a bridal suite. Great for business get-togethers, too: there are walks to the beach and the Helford river, so you can relax and unwind after a hard day's work! *No civil licence.*

Room hire	3: Board (max 20). Cabaret (max 50). Reception (max 80).
Catering	Approved & own caterers.
Sleeps	4 B&B.
Closed	Rarely.
Directions	Left at Red Lion in Mawnan Smith. After 0.5 miles right down Old Church Road. After 0.5 miles house on right through white gate immediately after Trerose Farm.

Tessa Phipps
Mawnan Smith, Falmouth TR11 5HX
Tel   +44 (0)1326 250784
Email   info@trerosemanor.co.uk
Web   www.trerosemanor.co.uk

The Rosevine

A super-smart bolthole on the Roseland peninsular with views that tumble across trim lawns and splash down to the sea. Come for celebrations and reunions, meetings and team-building, and out-of-this-world beachside weddings. Arrive by chauffeur-driven Volkswagen camper van, marry in the striking main dining room with its Lloyd Loom furniture and stunning sea views. Skip down to the beach at the bottom of the hill for a blessing, a fire-pit barbecue, a few atmospheric photos or just a spot of cricket. As darkness falls, make your way back to a luxurious tipi in the Brocklebank's semi-tropical garden and dance the night away. An eclectic choice for wedding breakfasts suggests tapas, posh fish and chips or three formal courses – simply prepared, beautifully presented. Children are welcomed with open arms: there's a playroom, an indoor pool, a trampoline, and babysitters and children's entertainers can be arranged. Tim and Hazel have created this small oasis with bright suites and apartments: expect airy bedrooms with uncluttered interiors. Messack comes with a gorgeous antique French bed and a private terrace.

Room hire	3 + marquee or tipi: Board (max 30). Cabaret (max 150). Theatre (max 50). Reception (max 150).
Catering	In-house & own caterers.
Sleeps	44: S/C or catered (max. 24 adults).
Closed	January.
Directions	From A390 south for St Mawes on A3078. Signed left after 8 miles. Right at bottom of road; just above beach.

Hazel & Tim Brocklebank
Rosevine, Portscatho, Truro TR2 5EW

Tel	+44 (0)1872 580206
Email	info@rosevine.co.uk
Web	www.rosevine.co.uk

The Vean at Caerhays Estate

Looking for an elegant grown-up house in which to hold a smart intimate wedding or a big occasion? Or are you after a peaceful hideaway for an all-important strategy meeting or awayday? The Vean – originally the vicarage attached to the castle – is ensconced on the stunning Caerhays Estate, and the renowned castle gardens are yours to enjoy. From the terrace you can lap up gentle bucolic views across the valley: a delightful spot for a marquee for a larger party. Inside, a sophisticated drawing room opens into a graceful dining room with a large gleaming table. The layout of this house lends itself beautifully to wedding receptions, celebration lunches, dinners, and formal meetings. The staff are quietly attentive and friendly, and you retire to thoroughly spoiling and individually designed bedrooms with long views over the grounds. Stay at least two nights if you can: you are less than a mile from long sandy beaches and there's heaps to do on the estate. Fling yourself, according to the season, into garden tours and garden lectures, game and clay-pigeon shooting, hunting and fishing. Marvellous.

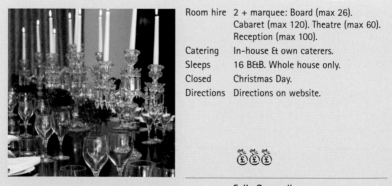

Room hire	2 + marquee: Board (max 26). Cabaret (max 120). Theatre (max 60). Reception (max 100).
Catering	In-house & own caterers.
Sleeps	16 B&B. Whole house only.
Closed	Christmas Day.
Directions	Directions on website.

Sally Gammell
Caerhays, Gorran, St Austell PL26 6LY

Tel	+44 (0)1872 500025
Email	enquiries@caerhays.co.uk
Web	www.thevean.co.uk

Trevalsa Court Country House Hotel

This Arts and Crafts house has a fine position at the top of the cliffs with views that run down to Cornwall's coastal path; a real seaside treat – friendly, stylish, seriously spoiling – with a log fire in an airy sitting room and sofas in a groovy bar. Best of all is the enormous mullioned window seat, a great place to sit and watch the weather spin by. John and Susan and their friendly staff will help make your party or wedding day perfect; you can marry in a pretty church at the bottom of the very steep hill, and sashay back for canapés and bubbly. Drop down to the beach for beautiful wedding photos. On fine days life spills onto the stone terrace amid beds of colour, with parties of up to sixty dining alfresco, or you can eat in the panelled dining room – in-house catering is divine, perhaps Cornish scallops or west country duck. Larger groups can eat and dance in a marquee on sprawling lawns. Bedrooms are lovely, all recently refurbished; they come in seaside colours with designer fabrics, the odd wall of paper, padded headboards and fancy bathrooms. Charming and exclusively yours. *Civil licence pending.*

Room hire	2 + marquee: Board (max 20). Cabaret (max 120). Reception (max 120).
Catering	In-house catering. Locally sourced.
Sleeps	24 B&B.
Closed	Mid-November to mid-February.
Directions	From St Austell, B3273, signed Mevagissey, through Pentewan to top of the hill, left at the x-roads, over mini r'bout. Hotel on left, signed.

Susan & John Gladwin
School Hill, Mevagissey,
St Austell PL26 6TH

Tel	+44 (0)1726 842468
Email	stay@trevalsa-hotel.co.uk
Web	www.trevalsa-hotel.co.uk

Boconnoc

A dramatic rhododendron- and camellia-lined drive leads to an obelisk, and views that sweep across parkland, ancient woods and a 15th-century church perching above the Georgian house. All kinds of events are held here, from the Cornwall Spring Flower Show in May to celebratory dinners, film shoots, product launches and conferences. Wedding receptions are special, and you can choose from the classical Drawing Room with its splendid panelling, or the light and airy Garden Room with French windows from which a marquee can be joined for larger parties. Dancing is in the red Victorian Smoking Room or panelled dining room; views from the terraced lawns are down the valley to the lake across from the deer park – perfect for romantic photographs. Civil ceremonies are held in the handsome Stable Yard, and guests can stay peacefully and comfortably in the Grooms' cottages or in The Tower; honeymooners can treat themselves to a four-poster in the main house. For candlelit dinners or sophisticated large receptions, this is a grand, fairytale setting – yet delightfully unpretentious.

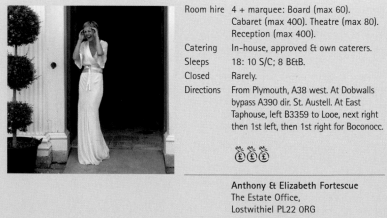

Room hire	4 + marquee: Board (max 60). Cabaret (max 400). Theatre (max 80). Reception (max 400).
Catering	In-house, approved & own caterers.
Sleeps	18: 10 S/C; 8 B&B.
Closed	Rarely.
Directions	From Plymouth, A38 west. At Dobwalls bypass A390 dir. St. Austell. At East Taphouse, left B3359 to Looe, next right then 1st left, then 1st right for Boconocc.

Anthony & Elizabeth Fortescue
The Estate Office,
Lostwithiel PL22 0RG

Tel	+44 (0)1208 872507
Email	adgfortescue@btinternet.com
Web	www.boconnocenterprises.co.uk

Lantallack Farm

The Georgian farmhouse stands on the side of a Cornish valley, apple orchards running away to the south, and farmland… there are pecking hens, horses, a pond of moorhens and paddling ducks, and a solar-heated swimming pool. Amazing views create a marvellous backdrop for a wedding or celebration, and you can have a marquee mounted on the lawn. The lovely old farm buildings and gardens create a playground of possibilities: marry under the wisteria walk or in the cart barn (with a cobbled floor and open front), or in Polly's Bower, a beautifully converted apple-crushing barn… or in the drawing or music rooms in the main house if the weather looks dodgy. Then it's off to the marquee, and the fun begins. Nicky, an artist, is as enthusiastic as she is meticulous – nothing is too much trouble, and that includes arrangements with caterers. There's no need to wave it all goodbye at the end of the day: bride and groom can retire to a swish open-plan suite in Polly's Bower while family and friends can B&B in the cosy farmhouse – or peacefully self-cater in Pippin Cottage, on the other side of the walled garden.

Room hire	5 + marquee. Cabaret (max 300). Theatre (max 300). Reception (max 300).
Catering	Approved caterers.
Sleeps	12: 4 B&B; 8 S/C.
Closed	Rarely.
Directions	A38 thro' Saltash, continue 3 miles. At Landrake 2nd right at West Lane. After 1 mile, left at white cottage for Tideford. House 150 yds on, on right.

Nicky Walker
Landrake, Saltash PL12 5AE

Tel	+44 (0)1752 851281
Email	enquiries@lantallack.co.uk
Web	www.lantallackweddings.co.uk

Ethical Collection: Environment; Community; Food. See page 208 for details

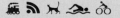

Pentillie Castle

Pentillie, in its castellated splendour, seduces you with its many temptations. It has acres of woodland gardens that tumble down to the river Tamar, and its own magnificent Bathing Hut – what a spot for informal parties! The great Victorian kitchen gardens, walled against the Cornish winds, await the restorer's spade, while Pentillie beef cattle graze in the fields on either side of the long drive up. There's an outdoor swimming pool heated by the sun, and a choice of different lawns to pitch a marquee (or three). As for the house, it's as handsome inside as the outside suggests. You have a choice of three lovely rooms to get married in, and a charming loggia. It's ideal for meetings too: everything you might need in a friendly house-party setting. Bedrooms are smart, spacious and deeply comfortable, and bathrooms pamper. Ted and Sarah, with their daughter Sammie, have mastered that delicate balancing act between luxury and stuffiness, bringing out one and banishing the other. Gasp at the loveliness of it all, then throw your shoes off before diving into the sofa.

Room hire	5 + marquee: Board (max 24). Cabaret (max. 250). Theatre (max 80). Reception (max 250).
Catering	In-house, approved & own caterers.
Sleeps	18 DB&B.
Closed	Rarely.
Directions	Cross Tamar River into Cornwall on A38. Right onto A388. 3.1 miles, then right at Paynters Cross. Entrance within 100 yds.

Sammie Coryton
St. Mellion, Saltash PL12 6QD

Tel	+44 (0)1579 350044
Email	contact@pentillie.co.uk
Web	www.pentillie.co.uk

Muncaster Castle

A narrow road snaking along the Lake District's delightful Esk Valley leads to this mellow-redstone castle. Parts of this striking Gothic pile – reputedly one of the UK's most haunted houses – go back to the 14th-century. The Penningtons, owners for 800 years, have opened five beautiful rooms, all licensed for weddings, so that visitors can share the dramatic setting. Perched on a hillside in 77 acres of woodland, the garden is a riot of rhododendrons, camellias and azaleas in spring. At the castle's heart is the Great Hall, epic in scale with stunning dark panelled walls, stained-glass windows and family portraits; the library, lined with 6,000 books and family ephemera, has gaspworthy views over the Lakeland Fells. The opulent drawing room, wood-panelled dining room and the toy soldier-filled Guard Room are also at your disposal; the converted stables and the granary suit informal parties and business groups. Warm, twinkly-eyed Sue helps you choose the best setting for your particular event. She also liaises with the in-house caterers – specialists in locally sourced and traditional food.

Room hire	4: Board (max 40). Cabaret (max 100). Theatre (max 120). Reception (max 100).
Catering	In-house catering.
Sleeps	126: 84 B&B; S/C 42.
Closed	Rarely.
Directions	Exit M6 at junc. 36, A590 for Barrow, right at Greenodd onto A5092 signed Whitehaven, join A595 to Muncaster.

Steve Bishop
Ravenglass CA18 1RQ
Tel   +44 (0)1229 717614
Email   info@muncaster.co.uk
Web   www.muncaster.co.uk

Nab Cottage

Rydal Water's mirrored surface and a dramatic backdrop of fells embrace this photogenic 500-year-old Lakes farmhouse. By comparison, the 18th-century stone barn – an eclectic small venue for workshops, celebrations, recitals – is positively modern. At one end, glass doors open onto a garden; at the other lies a sitting room; upstairs is for massages. Liz's décor is flirty and fun, a muddle of sparkly fabrics and ethnic knick-knacks, but for business meetings the place pulls its socks up. House parties take over the cottage's seven cosy bedrooms and sociable spaces, and the Opium Room is a veritable den, all purple shades, silk textiles and candles. If you're more traditional, try the fire-warmed sitting room or two dining rooms, one with a piano. Tim and Liz can whip up a meal for 20 on the Aga and are great with special diets. Rambling gardens conceal a summerhouse, sauna, paths tinkling with wind chimes and spots for al fresco dining; you can paddle around the lake in a Canadian canoe. Or choose a themed walking trail (river, lake, mountain, cave, waterfall, history). Quirky, authentic, and very chilled.

Room hire	1: Board (max 25). Cabaret (max 30). Theatre (max 30). Reception (max 30).
Catering	In-house catering.
Sleeps	18 B&B.
Closed	July, August & September.
Directions	From Windermere take A591 north, through Ambleside, through Rydal. Half way down Rydal Lake on right.

Tim & Liz Melling
Rydal, Ambleside LA22 9SD

Tel	+44 (0)1539 435311
Email	tim@nabcottage.com
Web	www.rydalwater.com

Linthwaite House Hotel & Restaurant

The view is magnificent: Windermere sparkles half a mile below and a chain of peaks rises beyond. Linthwaite is a grand Lakeland country house run in informal style by attentive and delightful staff. Everything is a treat. The function rooms with their gorgeous interiors (one decorated entirely with mirrors) create an alluring atmosphere for parties, while the buffets, barbecues and three-course wedding breakfasts are sublime. From a private party in the elegant deep-brown dining room to a less formal wedding in the groovy Billiard Room all is possible, and perfect. Spill onto the terrace for photos, bubbly and canapés, then swan around in 15 acres of trim lawns, formal gardens and wild rhododendrons. Stroll up through the bluebell wood to discover a small lake among the fields; fish, swim, retreat to the summerhouse and dream in the sun. They can lay on everything for meetings here, too – there's WiFi throughout, a flat screen for presentations, delicious working lunches. Do stay – gorgeous bedrooms are uncluttered and airy and those at the front have lake views. *Weekends minimum two nights.*

Room hire	3: Board (max 25). Cabaret (max 20). Theatre (max 54). Reception (max 50)
Catering	In-house catering.
Sleeps	62 DB&B.
Closed	Rarely.
Directions	M6 junc. 36. Take A590 north, then A591 for Windermere. At roundabout, left onto B5284. Past golf course and hotel signed left after 1 mile.

Mike Bevans
Crook Road, Bowness-on-Windermere,
Windermere LA23 3JA

Tel	+44 (0)1539 488600
Email	stay@linthwaite.com
Web	www.linthwaite.com

Gossel Ridding

You'd be forgiven for thinking you'd walked onto a film set. Every room has a view, every detail is perfect. Built in the 1880s, this heavenly, beautifully restored Arts & Crafts mansion sits above Lake Windermere, in a poetic land of water, wild fells and daffodils. Elegant touches fill every frame. Sweep into the grand oak-panelled hallway; soak up the lakeside panoramas; sip cocktails by a tinkling grand piano; dine by candlelight alongside carved panelling; chill out in the cinema room or steal into the snug. Cooking is a communal pleasure in a vast kitchen; later, cocoon yourself in delicious bedrooms and opulent bathrooms. This rare treasure cries out to be filled with life and laughter so invite family and friends to celebrate a smart wedding, a grand family occasion or simply a reunion of friends. Your discreet concierge service will help organise it all, including delicious menus from simple to sumptuous. Party in the spacious billiard room, add a marquee for extra space. Perfect too for get-away-from-it-all executive meetings: umpteen outdoor activity options are available to de-stress!

Room hire	3 + marquee: Board (max 20). Cabaret (max 60). Reception (max 120).
Catering	In-house & own caterers.
Sleeps	15 B&B. Whole house only.
Closed	Never.
Directions	Directions on website.

Fay Gorman Hext
Craig Walk,
Windermere LA23 2HT

Tel	+44 (0)7810 091008
Email	info@gosselridding.com
Web	www.gosselridding.com

Entry 31   Map 5

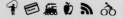

Augill Castle

A splendid folly castle built in 1841, happily situated between the Lake District and the Yorkshire and Durham Dales – and perfect for house parties and small weddings. Outside, 15 acres of lush gardens, dotted with moss-soft stone seating and a couple of elegant wrought iron gazebos. Inside, sumptuous interiors and furnishings create a wonderful sense of occasion: a stained-glass window on the staircase, a grand piano in the music room (licensed for civil ceremonies), ribbed ceilings, open fires, fine arched windows. A graceful dining room is the heart of the castle; gather here for wedding breakfasts, celebratory dinners and board meetings all under a magnificent vaulted ceiling. Team-building opportunities abound: cookery classes in the castle, falconry and archery in the grounds, quad biking and kayaking in the aptly named Eden Valley. The house is run informally: no uniforms, no rules, just Wendy, Simon and their staff to ply you with delicious food and drink. Dance the night away to a live band then trip upstairs to country-house bedrooms with beautiful beds, interesting art and boundless views.

Room hire	2: Board (max 24). Cabaret (max 46). Theatre (max 60). Reception (max 60).
Catering	In-house catering. Locally sourced.
Sleeps	28 B&B.
Closed	Never.
Directions	MG junc. 38; A685 through Kirkby Stephen. Just before Brough, right for South Stainmore; signed on left after 1 mile. K. Stephen railway station 3 miles.

🐾🐾🐾🐾🐾

Simon & Wendy Bennett
South Stainmore,
Kirkby Stephen CA17 4DE

Tel   +44 (0)1768 341937
Email   enquiries@stayinacastle.com
Web   www.stayinacastle.com

Ethical Collection: Environment; Community; Food. See page 208 for details

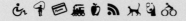

Greystoke Cycle Cafe

Your arrival at Greystoke village is the perfect end to a spectacular journey from Windermere via Kirkstone Pass and Ullswater – as any keen cyclist will tell you. Annie's home once served as wash house to Greystoke Castle next door, but she has done wonders with fresh plaster and modern art and now offers a small meeting venue – a café and cyclists' stop-off. Saunter down winding paths through a charming garden, passing eye-catching sculptures and a small yurt on the way, where 'quirky workshops' (ink painting, willow sculpting) are held. The main meeting room is to one side, stone-built with high ceilings, deep window ledges and wooden lintels; its airy well-lit interior seats up to 12. On sunny days you can lunch in the garden, but it's an equal treat to tuck into Annie's home-cooked and home-grown meals in the cheery farmhouse kitchen; there are fresh cakes and biscuits, too. Five miles from Penrith station, easily reached from the M6 by car or bike (but parking for cycle support vehicles only at the café), this is light years away from a corporate vibe. A super little place run by a friendly hostess.

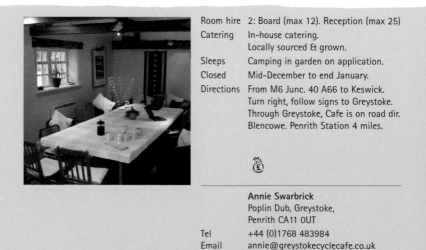

Room hire	2: Board (max 12). Reception (max 25)
Catering	In-house catering. Locally sourced & grown.
Sleeps	Camping in garden on application.
Closed	Mid-December to end January.
Directions	From M6 Junc. 40 A66 to Keswick. Turn right, follow signs to Greystoke. Through Greystoke, Cafe is on road dir. Blencowe. Penrith Station 4 miles.

Annie Swarbrick
Poplin Dub, Greystoke,
Penrith CA11 0UT
Tel   +44 (0)1768 483984
Email   annie@greystokecyclecafe.co.uk
Web   www.greystokecyclecafe.co.uk

Warwick Hall

Warwick Hall stands in 270 acres on the river Eden, facing east towards the hills and has one of the best salmon beats in the country. It may be only two miles from Carlisle but it's marvellously secluded. Cardinal Basil Hume used to fish here, and Bonnie Prince Charlie once stayed, though not in the comfort you can expect. Vast windows flood the house with light giving you a gem of a place for relaxed house parties, intimate weddings and very private business meetings or workshops. There's a magnificent hall for functions, a cavernous dining room for large supper parties, and a beautiful drawing room opening onto a terrace and a river of leaping fish. Bedrooms – some entered through a lovely rod room – have super beds, candles in the bathrooms, lots of books and fine views; the River Suite is romantic and gorgeous. Kind and friendly, Val has thought of everything: she can arrange florists, musicians, delicious home cooking or clever chefs, pre-wedding photo shoots, a marquee on the lawn... come and relish this inviting family home in all its splendour. *Alcohol licence pending.*

Room hire	4: Board (max 20). Cabaret (max 50). Theatre (max 80). Reception (max 120).
Catering	In-house, approved & own caterers.
Sleeps	16 B&B.
Closed	Rarely.
Directions	M6, junc. 43, then A69 east. After 2 miles, pass town sign and on left down hill before bridge.

Val Marriner
Warwick-on-Eden,
Carlisle CA4 8PG

Tel	+44 (0)1228 561 546
Email	info@warwickhall.org
Web	www.warwickhall.org

Manor Farm

Between two small dales, close to Chatsworth House, lies a cluster of medieval farms and church. Simon and Gilly, warm, delightful and enthusiastic about the history of their Grade II* listed house, love to host reunions, celebrations and meetings. Gilly's past experience in running events comes into its own and is applied to organising activities of all sorts: bush craft skills, arts and craft courses, workshops and educational visits. Meeting rooms, business facilities and break-out spaces with comfy sofas make this a great choice for most group activities and events; the Calf House can be adapted for social or business occasions and caterers can be recommended. Breakfast is served in the original Tudor kitchen, arched and atmospheric; food is scrumptious, local and organic. For sleeping, choose between the newly converted Hayloft, with big beamy bedrooms and huge beds, or cosy, pretty rooms in the house. Sitting within a designated World Heritage Site, the 200-acre hill farm offers masses of space and opportunities for outdoor activities galore. The pretty garden, with wonderful views, swoops to the distant river.

Room hire	1: Board (max 30). Cabaret (max 40). Theatre (max 50). Reception (max 50).
Catering	Approved & own caterers. Locally sourced.
Sleeps	12 B&B or S/C.
Closed	Rarely.
Directions	From M1 exit 28. A38 then A615 dir. Matlock. Thro' Wessington, after 1 mile right at Plough pub, then 3rd left. Down Dethick Lane 1 mile.

Ethical Collection: Environment; Community; Food. See page 208 for details

Simon & Gilly Groom
Dethick, Matlock DE4 5GG
Tel   +44 (0)1629 534302
Email   gilly.groom@w3z.co.uk
Web   www.manorfarmdethick.co.uk

Catton Hall

A grand South Derbyshire private house for countryphiles; its huge estate offers outdoor activities from hunting, shooting and fishing to carriage driving and ballooning; great team-building activities. A haha divides parkland from the formal garden; towering trees frame a magnificent and well-proportioned Georgian brick façade. Inside, charming Robin and Kate have created a warm, friendly, family home, full of unpretentious shabby chic. Relax with a drink in the stone-pillared entrance hall, watched over by ancestral portraits, after a busy day on the hills. In the sunny drawing, morning and dining rooms, marble fireplaces, chandeliers, antique furniture and dark oak floors under Persian rugs set a comfortable scene for meetings, house parties and family get-togethers. A sweeping oak staircase leads to a handful of grand bedrooms, with the requisite four-posters. Concoct a menu featuring delicious local produce with the in-house chef for small groups; for large events, held in a marquee, bring in outside caterers. Intimate marriage blessings take place in a Victorian chapel in the grounds. *No civil licence.*

Room hire	3: Board (max 30). Cabaret (max 50). Theatre (max 80). Reception (max 120).
Catering	Approved & own caterers.
Sleeps	16 DB&B.
Closed	Rarely.
Directions	From B'ham A38 dir. Derby, take A315 dir. Tamworth for 1 mile, left immed. after railway bridge. Catton Hall 1.5 miles on left after Lodge House.

Robin & Katie Neilson
Catton, Walton-on-Trent DE12 8LN

Tel	+44 (0)1283 716311
Email	r.neilson@catton-hall.com
Web	www.catton-hall.com

Little Barton

Artists and dreamers look no further. Few would not be inspired by the wild rugged landscape surrounding Little Barton — look past ramshackle farm buildings and over rolling pasture to Lundy Island and the shining sea. The main barn provides a large, rough and ready space for workshops, feasts and dancing. Owner Alex came to seek the good life and has been championing a relaxed approach to events ever since; you are actively encouraged to use the space imaginatively, and it is wonderful for those on a more modest budget. Greenies looking for a place to party or get married will rejoice, as all has been converted with Earth in mind. The self-catering is simple in unashamedly old-fashioned country style (hand-crafted beds, wooden floors), and you cook in kitchens equipped for large numbers. (Local cooks using well-sourced food can be called upon, too.) Best of all is the setting: the coast is a team-builder's dream, thanks to cliff walks, beaches and extreme sports minutes away. Come to embrace nature and all she represents… and the night skies and the sunsets are second to none. *No civil licence.*

Ethical Collection: Environment.
See page 208 for details

Room hire	2: Board (max 16). Cabaret (max 60). Reception (max 120).
Catering	Approved & own caterers. Locally sourced.
Sleeps	16 S/C or catered.
Closed	Rarely.
Directions	Off A39 for Hartland. Thro' village towards Hartland Quay. Left at Stoke then right for Elmscott at 1st signpost. First right down green lane.

Alex Wilkinson
Hartland, Bideford EX39 6DY

Tel	+44 (0)1237 441259
Email	enquiries@littlebartonhartland.co.uk
Web	www.littlebartonhartland.co.uk

Parnacott House

Bluebells and daffodils run riot, rhododendrons bloom, scented roses scramble over trellises, lavender and rosemary exude their fragrance... Enveloped by this floral cloud is a delightful Georgian home that owners John and Rondi love to let for celebrations, house parties and courses. Behind shuttered windows and gracious front rooms is the original 17th-century farmhouse, all flagstone floors and exposed beams, happily combining warmth with elegance. Host a dinner, a meeting or a course for up to 20 around a damask-draped dining table; across the hall, the drawing room gazes south towards Devon's rolling hills. Two bedrooms are at ground level, the other five pretty pastel rooms are upstairs; self-cater, arrange your own chef or ask Rondi to point you to a trusted caterer. What's more, the Vowlers positively encourage children and pets – where else can you find a kids' snug, a puppet theatre, dressing-up clothes and a barn with table tennis, rackets, croquet and boules? Not to mention endless tree-climbing possibilities in the 34-acre estate... So genuine, so peaceful, and such charming owners.

Room hire	1: Board (max 20).
Catering	Approved caterers. Locally sourced.
Sleeps	14 B&B or S/C. Whole house only.
Closed	Rarely.
Directions	Directions on booking.

Rondi & John Vowler
Holsworthy EX22 7JD
Tel   +44 (0)1409 253792
Email   rs@vowler.plus.com
Web   www.parnacotthouse.co.uk

Percy's Country Hotel

A meal at Percy's is no ordinary event – nor is a wedding or a party for that matter. Marry in the church, a hop and a skip down the road, or in the restaurant – an old beamed long house bedecked with flowers. This foodie-heaven restaurant with rooms is set on an organic farm that teems with life: pigs roam freely through 60 acres of woodland; Jacob sheep graze open pasture; geese, ducks and chickens supply the tastiest eggs. A kitchen garden is planted seasonally but much is harvested wild from the woods, a natural larder of mushrooms, juniper, crab apples and elderflower. Tina conjures up hog roasts, multi-course wedding breakfasts, buffets and vegetarian delights, served with the best English bubbly. Come for a stylish wedding, celebration or house party, where bedrooms are smart and spacious, food is organic and delicious, and eco awareness lies at the hotel's heart. They do meetings and cookery workshops too (game, fish, sausage making). Grab a pair of wellies and walk it all off on the huge estate… woodpeckers and kingfishers, deer and badger, old hedgerows, wild flowers and a wide sky await.

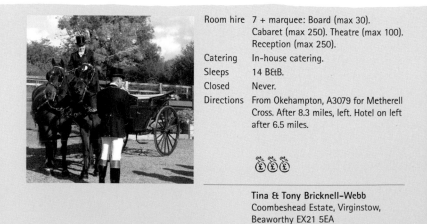

Room hire	7 + marquee: Board (max 30). Cabaret (max 250). Theatre (max 100). Reception (max 250).
Catering	In-house catering.
Sleeps	14 B&B.
Closed	Never.
Directions	From Okehampton, A3079 for Metherell Cross. After 8.3 miles, left. Hotel on left after 6.5 miles.

Tina & Tony Bricknell-Webb
Coombeshead Estate, Virginstow,
Beaworthy EX21 5EA

Tel   +44 (0)1409 211236
Email   info@percys.co.uk
Web   www.percys.co.uk

Shilstone

Rolling Devon countryside criss-crossed by dry stone walls, and not another house in sight. Shilstone has been lovingly restored with astounding attention to detail – even nails for door hinges are handmade copies of the originals. The interior is graceful and spacious, sun streaming through sash windows into panelled halls and airy rooms; drawing room and library are traditionally elegant, decked in subtle Farrow & Ball tones. This house is a blank canvas; guests are free to have exactly the event they want, from a wedding of any style to a weekend house party – or a business meeting or conference. Organise your own catering, or exploit a network of local connections to get the food of your dreams, even a personal chef. Sizeable bedrooms and bathrooms are stylish, full of architectural detail like original working fireplaces. West of the house, the old walled garden has endless views, space for a large marquee, and a fountain made from a grinding stone; the heated pool is nearby. A clutch of cottages and a converted barn with screening room and kitchen increase options for work and play. *Civil licence pending.*

Room hire	6: Board (max 50). Cabaret (max 160). Theatre (max 70). Reception (max 300).
Catering	Approved & own caterers.
Sleeps	Catered house for 15.
Closed	Rarely.
Directions	Exit A38 at Wrangton junction, left onto A3121, right at crossroads. Left at Texaco garage, Shilstone's stone gate posts 2 miles on left.

Sebastian Fenwick
Modbury, Ivybridge PL21 0TW

Tel	+44 (0)1548 830888
Email	seb.fenwick@virgin.net
Web	www.devonruralarchive.com

Dartington Hall

Gasp at the vastness and architectural magnificence of Dartington Hall: a collection of Grade I-listed medieval buildings enfolded by manicured gardens and a 1,000-acre estate that stretches languidly across South Devon countryside. Marry in the Upper Gatehouse, dodge a shower of confetti and stroll to the ancient formal gardens for photos, then saunter across to the Great Hall for a wedding breakfast. Dance under criss-crossing oak hammer beams and massive arched leaded windows. For festivals, concerts or conferences in the Great Hall you can set up a stage, tiered seating or full-on multimedia facilities with a support team. If that's too grandiose, a more intimate celebration or meeting can be magic'd up in one of several other rooms. For more informal dining there's the White Hart Restaurant, all flagstone floors and vaulted ceilings – gorgeous for candlelit dinners. Smart bedrooms lining the courtyard, a Barn Cinema for private viewing, the freedom to explore the estate's woodland and sculpture-dotted gardens… you have everything. Don't hold back.

Room hire	10: Board (max 28). Cabaret (max 120). Theatre (max 185). Reception (max 185).
Catering	In-house catering.
Sleeps	120 B&B.
Closed	Rarely.
Directions	Directions on website.

Helen Lynch
Dartington, Totnes TQ9 6EL

Tel	+44 (0)1803 847100
Email	bookings@dartingtonhall.com
Web	www.dartingtonhall.com

Fingals

Fingals is unique. Not so much a hotel, more the antithesis of a hotel, it's a big house with lots of bedrooms, run with fun and in laissez-faire style by energetic Richard and kind Sheila. Undeniably beautiful, Fingals is a handsome stone house, next to a stream in a little valley a mile or so from the Dart. Come for a few days for a relaxed and convivial house party, wedding or family celebration. Guests wander around as if at home, children and dogs mill about, tennis and games are played on the lawn. There's an indoor pool, a games room, sauna and jacuzzi, and books and pictures galore. Dinner is served in the wood-panelled dining room, a mellow and lovely space that encourages conversation; large parties flow through next door. Discuss menus with Richard – the food is local, seasonal, organic, delicious. The easy-going among us are happiest in this generous, engagingly chaotic place, where personality is more important than spotlessness. Rooms are eclectic, from the plainly traditional to the smart new eco suite. The Folly, a secluded two-storey hideaway, adds a touch of delightful eccentricity.

Room hire	4 + marquee: Board (max 40). Cabaret (max 150). Reception (max 150).
Catering	In-house catering.
Sleeps	35: 26 B&B; 9 S/C.
Closed	Mid-January to mid-March.
Directions	From Totnes, A381 south; left for Cornworthy. Right at x-roads for Cornworthy; right at ruined priory towards Dittisham. Down steep hill, over bridge. Sign on right.

Richard & Sheila Johnston
Dittisham, Dartmouth TQ6 0JA
Tel   +44 (0)1803 722398
Email   info@fingals.co.uk
Web   www.fingals.co.uk

Gurrow Point

Forget the Rolls and the horse and carriage – arrive by water instead! You could be married in Dartmouth two miles downstream and, tides permitting, travel by boat to your wedding breakfast. The more down-to-earth, but still attractive, approach to this spectacular peninsula is by car through the pretty village of Dittisham. Owned by the able and charming Peter and Sallie, Gurrow Point is an unforgettable spot: 80 acres of gently rolling fields and woodland looped about by the river Dart. You couldn't find a more private spot. There are just two houses – the main one, where Peter and Sallie live, and a self-catering cottage with its own delightful garden and access to the river. Events are held in a fabulously sited marquee, reached via an imposing long avenue of poplars, stretching through green-velvet parkland. This is a new venture and a barn is being built among the trees to house loos and the other practicalities, along with a professional kitchen for caterers. Guests are free to roam over most of the peninsula as well as the waterfront, and the family are on hand to advise with planning.

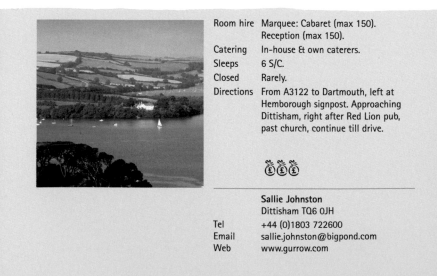

Room hire	Marquee: Cabaret (max 150). Reception (max 150).
Catering	In-house & own caterers.
Sleeps	6 S/C.
Closed	Rarely.
Directions	From A3122 to Dartmouth, left at Hemborough signpost. Approaching Dittisham, right after Red Lion pub, past church, continue till drive.

Sallie Johnston
Dittisham TQ6 0JH

Tel	+44 (0)1803 722600
Email	sallie.johnston@bigpond.com
Web	www.gurrow.com

The Great Barn

Plunge down a tunnel of arched trees to discover Devon's exclusive 'thatched cathedral': a threshing barn in medieval times, superbly 21st-century now. Banks of spotlights are tucked into the soaring ceiling, underfloor heating warms slate and elm floors, contemporary furniture sets off glowing lime-plastered walls. The clever layout means it can be as cosy for intimate weddings as for larger celebrations; the adjoining Roundhouse makes a great bar or children's room. Outside lies an enchanting walled garden, a riot of mature trees, roses and delicious corners – perfect for photos and drinks. Emma will help plan the day with a professionalism born of years producing live TV shows; John directs commercials and applies his lighting skills to your event with magnificent results. Everything is planned with precision: move from the ceremony to photos on the lawn, perhaps a glass of champagne (no corkage charge) then a slap-up meal. Guests can carry on dancing while you skip off to the Courtyard Cottage for the night. It's all yours, all fabulous, with the luxury of knowing it's in supremely competent hands.

Room hire	1 + marquee: Board (max 18). Cabaret (max 190). Theatre (max 220). Reception (max 300).
Catering	Approved caterers.
Sleeps	S/C cottage for 4.
Closed	Christmas & New Year.
Directions	Exit A38 at Teign Valley, join B3193. After golf course, right over stone bridge into Ashton. Continue 1 mile, Great Barn on left.

Emma & John Birkin
Place Barton, Higher Ashton,
Exeter EX6 7QP

Tel   +44 (0)1647 252552
Email   info@thegreatbarndevon.co.uk
Web   www.thegreatbarndevon.co.uk

Higher Westcott Farm

Urban chic floats through this ancient Devon longhouse, a tantalising blend of old cruck beams and fresh contemporary interiors. It's a super spot for a house party or a small summer wedding. The hamlet snoozes amid Dartmoor National Park's wild hills and handkerchief fields – a new home for Londoners Jo (a chef), Sam (graphic designer) and young George. The food is outstanding. In the dining room, Jo's beef and ale pie and brown bread ice cream appear deliciously alongside biodynamic wine. A fire crackles in the living room: pad over to the bar then settle on leather sofas. Or take a lazy afternoon in the sunny walled garden, the kids bounding over the lawn. Bedrooms have king-size beds dressed in percale and duckdown, swish bathrooms, and window seats gasping with views; in the loft is a lovers' bath under big oak beams. It's great for a house party for eight or a reception for 25; for more, set up a marquee. The moors call out to walkers, riders, fishermen (the day's catch will be served for supper). With just five houses in the hamlet, the only bright lights are the stars. *Dogs allowed in porch.*

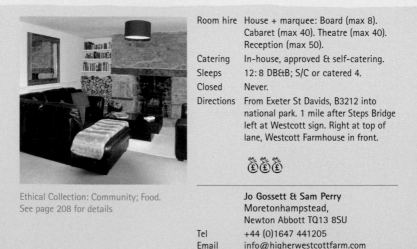

Room hire	House + marquee: Board (max 8). Cabaret (max 40). Theatre (max 40). Reception (max 50).
Catering	In-house, approved & self-catering.
Sleeps	12: 8 DB&B; S/C or catered 4.
Closed	Never.
Directions	From Exeter St Davids, B3212 into national park. 1 mile after Steps Bridge left at Westcott sign. Right at top of lane, Westcott Farmhouse in front.

Ethical Collection: Community; Food.
See page 208 for details

Jo Gossett & Sam Perry
Moretonhampstead,
Newton Abbott TQ13 8SU
Tel   +44 (0)1647 441205
Email   info@higherwestcottfarm.com
Web   www.higherwestcottfarm.com

The Old Rectory

In a pretty Devonshire village and protected by high walls, an early Victorian house with beautiful features, woodland views and five acres of grounds. In summer, marry outside in the romantic garden grotto, then twirl into a Mughal-style marquee. The house has had a stylish makeover: beautiful art, attractive sculptures, interesting touches at every turn, light flooding in from huge windows. Great for big house parties, there's a games room with a full-size snooker table, a well-equipped fitness room, a large sitting room with books and comfy sofas, and a dining room with a long table. Laurence, Leonie and their team know how to throw a party: they'll find jugglers, fire-eaters, jazz bands – anything to make it all go fizzingly. It's a relaxing, versatile place: you can run a workshop or meeting in the airy Yoga Barn, swim in the saltwater pool, take a solar-heated sauna. Springwater is purified, vegetables garden-grown and meat local. Upstairs are eight rather grand and spacious bedrooms, and more in the courtyard. And if those are not enough, there is overflow space in their two freehold pubs in the village.

Room hire	1 + 2 marquees: Board (max 26). Cabaret (max 150). Theatre (max 150). Reception (max 150).
Catering	In-house, approved & own caterers.
Sleeps	24 S/C. Camping available.
Closed	Rarely.
Directions	Past Red Lion Hotel, through main street. Left at the old blue pump, gates to house facing you.

Laurence & Leonie Delamar
Fore Street Hill, Chulmleigh EX18 7BS
Tel   +44 (0)1769 580123
Email   contact@theoldrectorychulmleigh.co.uk
Web   www.theoldrectorychulmleigh.co.uk

Hatswell Meadows

Ferns spill from hedgerows, ancient trees arch above and, at the end of the narrow lane, is a clearing where lawns sweep up to bluebell woods. Below is the salmon-rich river Exe; Hatswell lies in between. Bright and new, it has amber-warm stone walls, wood-framed windows, a gravel drive; inside, big rooms and lots of light. Marry in the gracious drawing room or the large hallway (a floor-to-ceiling window, a marble floor, a piano to provide musical accompaniment). Spill out into the rose garden for the reception, or spread onto the lawns. Make a grand entrance on the hand-crafted staircase, at the top of which big comfortable bedrooms lie. This is perfect for an intimate family wedding and you can stay on to relax, walk or fish – the owners have rights on the river. Bring your catch to the Aga – the spacious kitchen is the hub of the house. There's space galore plus a crafty conversion over the garage with a pool table and giant chess. Exmoor is close, and you're midway between the north and south Devon coasts. Perfect for team-building and awayday sessions, too. *No marquees.*

Room hire	2: Board (max 14). Theatre (max 40). Reception (max 40).
Catering	Own caterers & self-catering.
Sleeps	10 S/C.
Closed	Never.
Directions	M5 exit junc. 27; A361, 1st r'bout 3rd exit, first left, first left again and next left, house is first on right.

💰 💰

Wendy Edwards
Lower Washfield, Tiverton EX16 9PE

Tel	+44 (0)7795 100397
Email	contact@itsagreatcottage.co.uk
Web	www.itsagreatcottage.co.uk

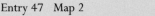

Loyton Lodge

It's hard to fault Loyton, a sublime country retreat. You're deep in the country, on the southern fringes of Exmoor, with commuting deer and strutting pheasants for company. The house is a dream, refurbished in exquisite country-house style. Enter a glass-walled hall, but wander at will and find excellent art in a beautiful drawing room, an enormous high ceiling'd dining room, French windows in the breakfast room. Marry in one of six licensed spaces, spill out into a gravelled courtyard, party in the billiard room or versatile dining room. And you get the whole place to yourself, with staff on hand to cook and clean. There's a vast bridal suite for summer weddings, while seriously indulgent bedrooms with sparkling bathrooms are fabulous and come in their own wing, an immaculate conversion of an old barn. Homemade food is excellent, with game from the estate and eggs from the farm; the flowers come from the garden. Perfect for intimate weddings, gatherings of family and friends or small meetings. Just ask for whatever you'd like – the charming Barnes family are on hand to help organise it all.

Room hire	5 + marquee: Board (max 25). Cabaret (max 34). Theatre (max 50). Reception (max 80).
Catering	In-house & approved caterers. Locally sourced.
Sleeps	Catered house for 20.
Closed	Rarely.
Directions	A396 to Bampton, right onto B3227. 1 mile, left at bridge. Over x'roads, left at hill, cont. 0.5 mile. On right.

Alick & Sally Barnes
Morebath, Tiverton EX16 9AS

Tel   +44 (0)1398 331051
Email   enquiries@loytonlodge.com
Web   www.loytonlodge.com

Huntsham Court

By the village church, Huntsham Court looks proudly over what was once the sprawling Ackland-Troyte estate: the grounds are now a neat five acres with croquet lawn and tennis court. Inside is evocatively Gothic: the Great Hall comes with dark wood and panelling, well-worn fabrics and big fireplaces; the Library has leather armchairs, a snooker table and noble portraits. The Drawing Room is lighter, with a great painted ceiling; and there's formality and elegance in the dining room. This is a relaxing space for big weddings and parties, where guests are left to their own devices; but note, David and Simone are reliably on hand with lists of caterers, and you have all the kitchen space you could need to feed the hungry hordes. Bedrooms – 27 in all – are warren-like, a happy mismatch of sizes and styles. A few have been modernised, others come with retro furniture; the Russian suites are bright and great fun. It's a place steeped in history and faded elegance, a wonderfully atmospheric bolthole for a murder mystery. Colonel Mustard and Miss Scarlet would not look out of place!

Room hire	5: Cabaret (max 120). Theatre (max 80). Reception (max 150).
Catering	Approved & own caterers.
Sleeps	66 S/C.
Closed	Never.
Directions	M5, junc. 27, A361 signed Barnstaple, exit immed. to Sampford Peverell, drive through, then right to Uplowman. Follow signs for 3 miles to Huntsham.

Simone & David Mills
Huntsham, Tiverton EX16 7NA
Tel   +44 (0)1398 361442
Email   enquiries@huntshamcourt.co.uk
Web   www.huntshamcourt.co.uk

Cadhay

Wisteria and roses scent the air as you explore your private kingdom – all yours for a wedding or family gathering. The flint and sandstone walls of this elegant Elizabethan manor enclose a historic courtyard ideal for outdoor dining; indoors, the Grade I-listed house is traditionally furnished and deeply comfortable. The pretty drawing room is licensed for small weddings; larger groups use the impressive 15th-century barrel-vaulted Roof Chamber or stately living room. The Garden Room in the grounds, rustic and relaxed, holds 60. Guests may roam the perfect English garden, complete with colourful borders, lily-strewn fishponds, and a lawn that calls out for a marquee for grand summer weddings. Inside, the formal dining room seats a score for smaller wedding breakfasts or family parties. Organise the caterers – Jayne is happy to advise. Bedrooms range from four-posters to child-friendly twins, and there are charming cottages too. Perfect for intimate winter weddings and family parties, this house has everything you need to go it alone, including a huge Aga-warmed kitchen. *Min. three to seven nights according to season.*

Room hire	5 + marquee: Board (max 22). Theatre (max 60). Cabaret (max 180). Reception (max 180).
Catering	Approved caterers.
Sleeps	34: S/C or catered house for 22. S/C cottages for 12.
Closed	January.
Directions	From M5 J29, A30 east, exit at Pattersons Cross. Follow signs for Fairmile, then Cadhay.

Jayne Covell
Ottery St Mary EX11 1QT

Tel	+44 (0)1404 813511
Email	jayne@cadhay.org.uk
Web	www.cadhay.org.uk

Combe House Devon

Combe is immaculate, an aristocratic Elizabethan manor house on a huge estate. Up a long drive, past Arabian horses running wild in the distance, you pull up at a place of architectural splendour; greet your guests in a wonderfully atmospheric hall. The Panel Room transforms from an elegant meeting room by day to a gracious, glowing space for dining or relaxing by night; the green Mural Room, a fantasy of country scenes with huge views, is just the ticket for a larger party. A sitting room/bar in racing green opens onto a croquet lawn for informal fun and games; and intimate meals by candlelight are served in the restored Georgian Kitchen. Everything is done beautifully here: Ruth and Ken help you plan your event, be it wedding, house party or meeting, while a battalion of staff attends to every detail. Sumptuous meals are prepared from the finest local ingredients, the Victorian kitchen gardens providing much for the table. Bedrooms are fabulous: stately fabrics, wonderful beds, gorgeous bathrooms, outstanding views. Come for total privacy and seclusion, or pull out all the stops for a really special occasion!

Room hire	3 + marquee: Board (max 26). Cabaret (max 150). Reception (max 150).
Catering	In-house catering.
Sleeps	40 B&B or DB&B.
Closed	Rarely.
Directions	From M5 exit 29 to Honiton. Leave A30 at Honiton for Heathpark and Gittisham. Hotel signed in village.

Ruth & Ken Hunt
Gittisham, Honiton EX14 3AD

Tel	+44 (0)1404 540400
Email	stay@combehousedevon.com
Web	www.combehousedevon.com

The Old Kennels

A tranquil pastoral setting, for holistic workshops, musical gatherings and weekend retreats. The Old Kennels, built in the 19th century for the Axevale Hunt, stand beneath an ancient spreading oak in a distant corner of Boswell's Farm, with far-reaching rolling views. Reached by a country lane from the busy Lyme Regis road, it's a plain brick building, newly renovated to create two white-walled studios divided by sliding doors, with modern sprung flooring and old beams. They're not huge rooms, but calm, warm and flooded with natural light. There's a small kitchen, so you could do your own simple event catering, but efficient Linda can supply a list of local people. The Pavilion, a wooden summerhouse, is used for meditation or massage: Linda is passionate about alternative health therapies and runs pilates courses. You can stay on the farm, in traditionally decorated, self-catering cottages in an attractive collection of farm buildings, and have the run of 45 acres of the lovely Sweetcombe Valley — hedgerow walks, the Snod brook. Or walk to the sea at Sidmouth, just two miles away. *No civil licence.*

Room hire	2: Board (max 30). Cabaret (max 30). Theatre (max 40). Reception (max 60).
Catering	Approved & own caterers.
Sleeps	36 S/C.
Closed	Never.
Directions	Exeter A3052 to Sidmouth. At Sidford left Harcombe Lane East. At Harcombe Cross turn left, 0.1 miles turn right at large gateway, lane to building.

Linda Dillon
Sidford, Sidmouth EX10 0PP

Tel   +44 (0)1395 514162
Email dillon@boswell-farm.co.uk
Web   www.boswell-farm.co.uk

Upcott House

Upcott is an Arts and Crafts gem in a wonderful setting, perfect for workshops, small weddings and celebrations. This big rambling house with its own little turret has been revived by Liz and Malcolm in an eco-friendly way: local stone and timbers have been sought, original boards revealed, walls smoothed and eco-tinted in subtle colours, and discreet spot lighting added – along with the odd glistening chandelier. Stained-glass windows and period detail rub shoulders with slick leather sofas, funky fabrics and contemporary pieces. The spacious and informal living room has a wood-burning stove and guests can spill out onto the veranda. The oak table in the dining area seats 12; the kitchen is sleek and designed for special dinners; and the workshop room, with TV, WiFi and baby grand, is for cosier groups. Comfortable bedrooms, one with a balcony, another a turret, have blissful views; super bathrooms have hot water generated by hidden solar panels. Lawns slope to the garden's edge, the sparkling sea sweeps beyond, and Liz and Malcolm are on hand with all the suppliers you need. *No civil licence. No marquees.*

Room hire	Whole house: Board (max 12). Reception (max 25).
Catering	Approved & self-catering.
Sleeps	12 S/C.
Closed	Never.
Directions	From Seaton B3174 towards Beer. After 0.25 miles left into Old Beer Road, signed Seaton Hole. Upcott immed. on right after road widens.

Ethical Collection: Environment; Food.
See page 208 for details

Liz & Malcolm Robinson
Old Beer Road, Seaton, Beer EX12 2PZ

Tel	+44 (0)1297 20307
Email	stay@devonretreat.com
Web	www.devonretreat.com

River Cottage HQ

If you aren't familiar with River Cottage from Hugh Fearnley-Whittingstall's books and TV series then you're in for a surprise. The 300-year-old Devon longhouse sits on an organic farm, so look out for saddleback pigs, Red Devon cows, chickens and geese. It's deeply rural and guests arrive by tractor! Wedding parties and dinners mostly take place in the warm, arty interior of a beautifully converted threshing barn; chefs pop in and out of the kitchen and up to 64 guests sit sociably around two large oak tables. It's equally good for courses: practise jam-making, curing or foraging; build a clay oven; request a tailormade course or hold your own. Small meetings use the cosy farmhouse dining room; larger parties and conferences spill out to a marquee. It goes without saying that the food here is fabulous, local, seasonal and organic, be it a spit roast or a gourmet tasting. Enjoy pre-dinner drinks in a Mongolian yurt that glimmers with fairy lights. Green thinking is at the heart of it all and the exuberance, friendliness and flexibility of the staff shows. A magical setting for a pretty special place. *No civil licence.*

Room hire	2 + yurt + marquee: Board (max 16). Cabaret (max 250). Theatre (max 250). Reception (max 250).
Catering	In-house catering.
Closed	Christmas & New Year.
Directions	Directions on booking. Railway station at Axminster.

Catherine Bugler
Axminster EX13 8TB

Tel	+44 (0)1297 630302
Email	cat@rivercottage.net
Web	www.rivercottage.net

Ethical Collection: Environment; Community; Food. See page 208 for details

Chaffeymoor Grange

This striking and much-loved 17th-century manor house is an exceptional place for strategic get-togethers, atmospheric house parties, elaborate celebrations and modish weddings. Tucked away from the usual hubbub, it's all laid on here – state-of-the-art presentation equipment; a personal chef to spoil you with dinners and hampers; WiFi throughout. Bright, bold furnishings combine with noble old beams; the compact boardroom is perfect for ten and the graceful dining room takes twice as many for meetings and celebratory dinners. Outside you have the run of five acres – clay shooting and archery; treasure hunts to a backdrop of tinkling fountains; a small rowing lake; tennis on the private court and croquet on the lawn. Later, let the Oak Room's elegant panelling embrace you; a huge stone fireplace and wood-burner, deep sofas, bucket chairs, fresh flowers – all invite you to get cosy. Or draw the day to a perfect close, twirling under the stars on terraced lawns. A lovely welcome, timeless elegance and ample and stylish bedrooms with heavenly views combine to make this a memorable venue.

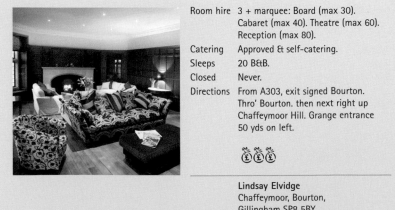

Room hire	3 + marquee: Board (max 30). Cabaret (max 40). Theatre (max 60). Reception (max 80).
Catering	Approved & self-catering.
Sleeps	20 B&B.
Closed	Never.
Directions	From A303, exit signed Bourton. Thro' Bourton. then next right up Chaffeymoor Hill. Grange entrance 50 yds on left.

Lindsay Elvidge
Chaffeymoor, Bourton,
Gillingham SP8 5BY

Tel	+44 (0)1747 841396
Email	info@chaffeymoorgrange.com
Web	www.chaffeymoorgrange.com

West Axnoller

Breathtaking contrasts slice through this rural Dorset scene. Views roll down towards the wild Jurassic Coast while West Axnoller fizzes with colour, texture and state-of-the-art sumptuousness. If the breeze doesn't blow you away, these three houses will; each displays country living at its most stylishly pampering. Axnoller, the place for weddings, celebrations and executive meetings or training sessions, looks every bit the grand farmhouse with its stone walls and sash windows, while inside is a surprisingly theatrical blend of period and modern pieces: lacquered chests, fruitwood tables, porcelain lamps… Voltaire and Burggraaf are similarly jazzy and contemporary, with open-plan sitting, dining and kitchen areas (where cookery courses take place), and plush, bright bedrooms. Each house has a private garden and heated pool, sauna and steam room, and a gym, games room and hot tub. You can sleep 36 for a fully catered celebration; or choose between Axnoller for B&B and Burggraaf and Votaire for self-catering. Alo can arrange it all – from a butler to a full-blown bells-and-whistles wedding. *Min. stay three nights.*

Room hire	3 + marquee: Board (max 25). Cabaret (max 200). Theatre (max 75). Reception (max 200).
Catering	In-house & approved caterers.
Sleeps	36: Catered house for 12. Two S/C or catered houses, each for 12.
Closed	Rarely.
Directions	Directions on website.

Alo Brake
West Axnoller Farm,
Beaminster DT8 3SH

Tel	+44 (0)1308 861744
Email	enquiries@stayinstyleuk.com
Web	www.stayinstyleuk.com

Peek House

What a place for a house party, or an anniversary, or a bridal party: here is luxury, space and natural magnificence! Within its landscaped grounds and its grand Victorian mansion, Rousdon Estate has it all – in hatfuls. Plus… a private beach, a nature reserve, a cinema, games rooms and stunning sea views. Peek House, the old servants' wing, is sumptuously renovated, so float through rooms dressed in rich colours, fine fabrics and designer wallpapers, collapse into deep leather sofas or perch on exquisitely carved Balinese furniture, wend your way up lushly carpeted stairs wrapped around a leafy wrought-iron pillar. Billiard House is just as eye-catching with its intricate woodwork, painted ceiling and original cupola – fabulous for a concert or presentation. Take either or both for a party or a corporate event. The mahogany table in Peek House seats 18, and there's a sitting room to retire to, and gardens; catering is easily arranged. When the evening ends, sink into soft, dreamy beds, dreaming of clifftop walks and reviving massages. You'll find all the trimmings here. *No civil licence.*

Room hire	3: Board (max 18). Reception (max 30).
Catering	Approved & self-catering.
Sleeps	19 S/C.
Closed	Never.
Directions	A358 from Axminster dir. Seaton; left at Boshill Cross onto A3052 dir. Lyme Regis; continue to Rousdon. Direct rail link Axminster to London.

Judith Ellard
Rousdon Estate, Lyme Regis DT7 3XR
Tel   +44 (0)1297 444734
Email   judith@peekhouse.co.uk
Web   www.peekhouse.co.uk

Glenthorne

With its elegant cast-iron veranda wrapped in wisteria, this attractive Victorian villa has terraced gardens that face the boat-bobbed waters of Portland Bay: a 2012 Olympics events' panorama will unfold right here. A former rectory with original tiles and oak staircases, vibrant colours and ornate mahogany, this is a dramatic venue for large house parties and family celebrations; while pre-wedding guests — and bride and groom — can take over the entire house, plus the apartments in the garden. The sitting room glows at night with tall lamps, brilliant red walls, polished silver, a chaise longue, glass baubles dangling over a mirror... you're all set for a murder mystery! The dusky pink dining room seats 12 for dinner or a meeting; a large sitting/dining room sports red leather sofas and modern art. The house has a well-equipped kitchen and roomy bedrooms, three of the smaller newly decorated attic rooms having fabulous views. There's a heated pool, a trampoline and table tennis, and Olivia can arrange water sports for team-building. Launch your boat from the secret sandy cove below, revel in the setting.

Room hire	2: Board (max 22).
Catering	Own caterers & self-catering.
Sleeps	S/C or catered house & apartments for 25.
Closed	Rarely.
Directions	A354 Weymouth to Portland, 0.5 miles to top of hill. As road bears right, left into Old Castle Road. Follow signs to house. Direct railway line to Waterloo 1 mile.

Olivia Nurrish
15 Old Castle Road, Weymouth DT4 8QB

Tel	+44 (0)1305 777281
Email	info@glenthorne-holidays.co.uk
Web	www.glenthorne-holidays.co.uk

Higher Melcombe Manor

Leave Dorset's winding lanes behind and draw up before a gracious, charming and exquisitely romantic 16th-century manor house, guarded by giant limes. Inside you have a choice of exceptional rooms to marry in, including the Great Hall – vaulted, filled with light (note the spectacular stained-glass window) and perfect for up to 100 guests... and you can choose your own caterers. The cosy dining room, with its log fire and long oak table, suits smaller weddings or celebratory dinners. The drawing room (also licensed for civil ceremonies), elegant with antiques, sprinkled with china and silverware, overlooks an enchanting garden, all sweeping lawns, secret paths and benches dotted about for sunny mornings and dazzling sunsets. Brides can dress in the Monks Room off the Great Hall – and later sleep in the very fine Panelled Room; the stylish simplicity extends to the attic. Gracious Lorel, who loves to entertain, and charming Michael are still working on this huge inherited project. Their deliciously elegant home is all yours for a day, a night, a weekend – whatever takes your fancy.

Room hire	3: Board (max 14). Cabaret (max 50). Reception (max 100).
Catering	Approved & own caterers.
Sleeps	6 B&B.
Closed	Christmas.
Directions	From Dorchester, A35, Piddlehinton exit (B3142). Left to Cheselbourne, right into Long Lane. Cont. 5 miles to crossroads at Melcombe Bingham, then left.

Lorel Morton & Michael Woodhouse
Melcombe Bingham DT2 7PB

Tel	+44 (0)1258 880251
Email	lorel@lorelmorton.com
Web	www.highermelcombemanor.co.uk

Plumber Manor

Easy to see why the Olympic rowing team meet here every year. Once inside the grand stone house, lost with its dreamy mullions down Dorset's sleepy lanes, you are left in peace amidst huge flagstones, open fires, oil paintings, well-worn rugs and napping labradors. If designer chic is your thing, stay away: but some will adore the floral wallpapers and antiques in large, light bedrooms (in the main house or in converted barns) and the dated-but-immaculate bathrooms. Come for local beef, lamb and game and the hale and hearty surroundings, be adventurous in 60 acres of lawns, fields and woodland with the river Develish rushing through, or just sit idly on the terrace and watch. Kind June can be summoned when you need her for anything from flowers to projectors to a surprise birthday cake; comfort is the key and you'll get the place to yourselves whether you are holding a family celebration, house party, small meeting or conference. There are plenty of places to hide in any case, and the biggest velvet sofa you will ever see on the first-floor landing. Your sleep should be deep.

Room hire	2: Board (max 14). Cabaret (max 44). Theatre (max 25). Reception (max 75).
Catering	In-house catering.
Sleeps	32 B&B.
Closed	February.
Directions	West from Sturminster Newton on A357. Across traffic lights, up hill & left for Hazelbury Bryan. Follow brown tourism signs, hotel signed left after 2 miles.

💷💷💷

Richard, Alison & Brian Prideaux-Brune
Plumber, Sturminster Newton DT10 2AF

Tel	+44 (0)1258 472507
Email	book@plumbermanor.com
Web	www.plumbermanor.com

Deans Court

A hidden gem on the fringes of Wimborne, a stone's throw from the minster, this house has been in Sir William's family since 1548. Today the formal 18th-century façade of brick and stone complements a grand Georgian interior: huge rooms adorned with Persian rugs, mahogany, oak and the soft gleam of old velvet. Time stands still. The formal dining room, its cerise walls lit by immense windows, is great for meetings, while the stately hall makes an elegant backdrop for recitals. Wedding guests pass through the house to the remarkable garden: 13 tranquil, informal acres of lawn, woodland, orchard and kitchen garden bordering meadows and the trout-laden river Allen. Exotic and venerable trees – from Mexican Swamp Cypress and a tulip tree planted in 1606 to gnarled mulberries by the Saxon pond – can be illuminated for evening receptions. Marquees of any size (for up to 500), including two beautiful Moroccan circular tents, are sited to suit you; ask efficient Ali for details of local caterers. Two farm cottages undergoing restoration will soon provide self-catering accommodation for 8. *Civil licence pending.*

Room hire	3 + 3 marquees: Board (max 20). Cabaret (max 75). Theatre (max 500). Reception (max 1,000).
Catering	In-house, approved & own caterers. Locally sourced.
Closed	2 weeks in September.
Directions	M27 west from M3, then A31. Follow signs for Dorchester, Wimborne, then Town Centre. Left at East St. into Deans Court Lane, gate on right.

William Hanham
Wimborne BH21 1EE

Tel	+44 (0)1202 880515
Email	estateoffice.deanscourt@googlemail.com
Web	www.deanscourt.org

Maison Talbooth

How's this for getting your wedding – or hen or house party – off with a splash? An outdoor, tropically heated pool with swish Pool House, and a hot tub for extra bubbles. Throw in a poolside afternoon tea, cocktails and canapés (there's a log-burning stove to keep off the chill), spa treatments... you could get used to this. Maison Talbooth is full of surprises and theatrical touches. Climb the steps of the handsome Victorian rectory to a cool contemporary drawing room with bold lighting and creamy sofas, then through to a high-vaulted Garden Room with peerless views over Constable country. If it's a small party, you can marry in the former and celebrate in the latter, with drinks on the terrace or lawn. Bigger parties and receptions can be whisked (one minute down the road) to the sister property, Le Talbooth, with a glorious riverside setting and a choice of river-view dining terrace or marquee. Back at base, you can dance in the Garden Room before slipping away to gorgeous cream-on-cream bedrooms (some with hot tubs). Thoughtful touches, genuine staff. It's a fun way to celebrate in style.

Room hire	2: Board (max 24). Cabaret (max 50). Reception (max 50).
Catering	In-house catering.
Sleeps	Catered house for 24.
Closed	Never.
Directions	North on A12 past Colchester. Left to Dedham, right after S bend. Maison Talbooth is on right, follow brown signs.

Gerald, Diana & Paul Milsom
Stratford Road, Dedham,
Colchester CO7 6HN
Tel   +44 (0)1206 322367
Email   maison@milsomhotels.com
Web   www.milsomhotels.com

Frampton Court Estate

A hidden jewel, this magnificent Grade I-listed house is set in acre upon acre of idyllic countryside. The manor of Frampton-on-Severn has been in the family since the 11th-century and owners Rollo and Janie care deeply about this much-loved estate. Grand gates sweep you into glorious parkland; mist wraps round trees, sunshine glints on the lake. Inside, the Court is packed with treasures: fine examples of decorative woodwork, delicate porcelain and ancestral portraits. House parties use the grand Hall with cheerful log fire, plus the elegant morning and dining rooms; great for meetings too. Helpful manager Gillian organises breakfast and can conjure up dinner for groups of up to 20. Or self-cater in the spacious, exquisitely pretty Gothic-style Orangery, with its spiral staircase and octagonal shaped rooms, overlooking the lily-strewn ornamental canal. Wedding receptions are hosted in the park or in the impressive timber-framed Wool Barn; with mezzanine gallery and clever lighting, this is perfect for both parties and exhibitions. Graceful, comfortable bedrooms have views over the estate. *No civil licence.*

Room hire	5+ marquee: Board (max 14). Cabaret (max 400). Theatre (max 40). Reception (max 500).
Catering	In-house & own caterers.
Sleeps	18: 10 B&B; 8 S/C.
Closed	Rarely.
Directions	M5 junc. 13, A38 south, right onto B4071. Left down village green. Orangery and Frampton Court on left, Wool Barn on right. Railway station Stonehouse.

Janie Clifford
Frampton-on-Severn GL2 7EP

Tel   +44 (0)1452 740698
Email   events@framptoncourtestate.co.uk
Web   www.framptoncourtestate.co.uk

Owlpen Manor

Perched on a wooded hillside in a hidden Cotswold valley is one of England's finest Tudor manors. Inside is the Manders' family home, a warm symphony of muted colours, lovely antiques and sumptuous, well-worn fabrics. With an exquisite Victorian church for marriage ceremonies or blessings, this delightfully informal set up just six miles from Tetbury could be all yours for a romantic wedding weekend – or a week. Whether your guests number 20 or 200, efficient, adaptable Lady Mander and her team organise it all, from spit-roasts to formal wedding breakfasts or anything your heart desires. Hold intimate celebrations in the small but perfectly formed Great Hall or in the charmingly cruck-beamed Cyder House; spread into marquees on the lawns for larger gatherings. Wedding photos among the box parterres and topiaried yews of the garden are a must. The manor, its 125-acre estate and its lovely holiday cottages can also be hired for meetings, conferences and parties. As for Lady Mander's popular Cyder House Restaurant, its menu bursts with Owlpen game and beef, and produce from the Elizabethan garden. *No civil licence.*

Room hire	2 + 2 marquees: Board (max 12). Cabaret (max 48). Theatre (max 60). Reception (max 200).
Catering	In-house catering.
Sleeps	40 S/C.
Closed	Never.
Directions	One mile east of Uley, off the B4066. Follow signs from the small green past the Old Crown pub in Uley (opposite the church).

Jayne Simmons
Dursley GL11 5BZ

Tel	+44 (0)1453 860261
Email	sales@owlpen.com
Web	www.owlpen.com

The Kingscote Barn

Spring lambs gambol in the grassy valley enveloping this 400-acre farm; at its centre, a Cotswold stone barn glows in its new role as party venue. Guests congregate in the glass and stone-walled reception space, and sip drinks from a bar set up in the antechamber; then it's off to the main room to party, beneath aged arched beams and metal chandeliers: a striking space. Those who need a break from the dance floor can scamper up to the mezzanine gallery for a bird's-eye view, or slip out to the terrace or the courtyard; in good weather the lawn makes a stunning setting for photographs – and hog roasts. Meals appear from a spotless stainless steel kitchen and the Barn charges no corkage for your wine. The space is just as suitable for more sober meetings, with the added option of activities such as clay-pigeon shooting. And if you don't fancy driving home in the dark, nip over to the sweet Spring Cottage for the night, or upstairs to Tallet House. Kingscote is perfect: simple, flexible, well-run and welcoming, with beautiful Gloucestershire views. *Experienced event co-ordinators on site.*

Room hire	3: Board (max 30). Cabaret (max 140). Theatre (max 150). Reception (max 200).
Catering	Approved caterers. Locally sourced.
Sleeps	10: 4 B&B; 6 S/C.
Closed	Christmas.
Directions	Directions on website.

Richard Gale
Binley Farm, Kingscote,
Tetbury GL8 8YE

Tel	+44 (0)1453 861161
Email	info@kingscotebarn.co.uk
Web	www.kingscotebarn.co.uk

Matara Centre

Tucked away in rolling Cotswold countryside is Matara, an oasis that calls your heart to sing and your spirits to soar. Geoffrey has created an east-west fusion of tranquil, contemplative spaces, and has facilitated a rare energy for deep thinking and reflective action. Groups working to achieve a common objective, be it for a social purpose or a mission-driven organisational goal, will be inspired. Matara is ultra-green, too. The Hillarium, with its star-studded dome ceiling, is perfect for an 'open space' meeting: Indian statues and ethnic rugs and hangings are set off by high beamed ceilings, flagstone floors and an Italian Renaissance door. In the beautiful cloistered courtyard are an ancient beech and a tinkling fountain; beyond, arbours and cobbled walkways to a Japanese-styled garden. All doors open onto 28 meandering acres of gardens or woodland: discover a wishing tree, sculptures, a pond bursting with wildlife. Stay in the centre's 'zen' rooms or in the crisp fresh rooms of Kingscote House, or in the pretty lodge in the Chinese tea garden. A delicious mix of style and soul – and wonderful for weddings too.

Room hire	9: Board (max 50). Cabaret (max 150). Theatre (max 90). Reception (max 200).
Catering	Approved caterers. Local & organic where possible.
Sleeps	24 B&B.
Closed	Rarely.
Directions	From M5 junc. 13, A419, A46, A4135 dir. Dursley, Matara on right. From M4 junc. 18, A46 N 11 miles, Matara on left.

Geoffrey Higgins
Kingscote Park,
Tetbury GL8 8YA
Tel   +44 (0)1453 861050
Email   geoffrey@matara.co.uk
Web   www.matara.co.uk

Ethical Collection: Environment; Community. See page 208 for details

Abbey Home Farm

'Sustainability' sums up the ethos of this lively organic demonstration farm, the scene of your eco-friendly conference, meeting, workshop, party, wedding reception – anything, as long as you want the organic touch. Choose your space in the Green Room or Verandah Café, a model of environmental self-sufficiency: solar panels, woodchip boiler, recycled timber, its own bore hole… a welcoming, homely space with pretty green paintwork and striking Indian touches. Hop next door to the well-stocked farm shop and café for a delicious organic lunch or coffee – they're great with veggie meals and cakes – while gazing across the fields where your meal was grown. How about a blessing at the stone circle followed by a hog roast; or a cookery workshop or Masterchef event in the Teaching Kitchen? Or even a team-building event in the eco camp of yurts – certainly unique. Hilary and her team exude competence but are also flexible and love providing those extras that make for a perfect day, from home-grown organic flowers to scrumptious meals. A veritable organic oasis in the heart of the Cotswolds. *No civil licence.*

Room hire	2: Board (max 30). Cabaret (max 180). Theatre (max 180). Reception (max 200).
Catering	In-house catering. Fully organic, mainly local.
Sleeps	179: S/C yurts for 23. S/C cottage for 4. S/C hut for 2. S/C camping for 150.
Closed	25-26 December; 1 January.
Directions	From Cirencester B4425 dir. Burford, straight on at lights. Signs on left to Organic Farm Shop. Train Kemble 7 miles.

Hilary Chester-Master
Burford Road,
Cirencester GL7 5HF

Tel	+44 (0)1285 640441
Email	info@theorganicfarmshop.co.uk
Web	www.theorganicfarmshop.co.uk

Cripps Barn

The immense fireplace, flagged floors and oak joists spanning high stone walls reveal the care that the owners put into this characterful 18th-century barn near Cirencester. Its rustic charm hides a range of modern essentials – coloured lights and glitter ball for discos, an iPod docking station for DIY music, and full DJ paraphernalia. A permanent marquee, its tented ceiling lit by chandeliers, is reached through a large side door; in tandem with the barn it provides table and seating layouts for numerous events, from wedding ceremonies to dinner and dancing. Across the barn, double doors open to a terrace and pleasingly informal garden where flares, lanterns and a bonfire glow after dark. A stand of trees conceals secluded seating and a bosky glade; guests can camp in the grounds if they choose. Gifted chef Mark Stone does all catering in-house using prime local and seasonal ingredients; his speciality is whole lamb roasted outside, Argentina style, on an enormous barbecue. Jenny looks after the details; working efficiently together, Felicity and her team can organise every aspect of your event.

Room hire	1 + marquee: Cabaret (max 160). Reception (max 160).
Catering	In-house catering.
Closed	January.
Directions	From Cirencester B4425 to Bibury, take Foss Cross turning on left before entering Bibury. Cripps Barn 1.5 miles on left. Directions on website.

€€€

Felicity Henriques
Fosscross Lane, Bibury,
Cirencester GL7 5ND

Tel	+44 (0)1285 740035
Email	enquiries@crippsbarn.com
Web	www.crippsbarn.com

The New Inn at Coln

The New Inn is old – 1632 to be exact – but well-named nonetheless: a top-to-toe renovation has swept away past indiscretions and any hint of stuffiness. These days, it's all rather smart. The pub stands in a handsome Cotswold village with peaceful views across water meadows to the river; delightful walks start from the front door, so spread your wings. Ivy roams on original stone walls and a sun-trapping terrace where roses bloom in summer. Inside, airy interiors come with low ceilings, painted beams, flagged floors and fires that roar. Come for a seriously pampering celebratory get-together with family and friends; have it all to yourselves for the weekend and feast on delicious meals prepared by the in-house team, anything from a barbecue to a five-course dinner. Warmly elegant bedrooms are a treat, all quirkily luxurious. Or hold a small meeting in the well-equipped meeting room with its own patio – perfect for a private working lunch or a cosy drinks party. The New Inn is popular for intimate weddings too, and Stuart prides himself on getting things just right for you, whatever your choice.

Room hire	2: Board (max 12). Cabaret (max 34). Theatre (max 14). Reception (max 80).
Catering	In-house catering.
Sleeps	26 B&B.
Closed	Rarely.
Directions	From Oxford, A40 past Burford, B4425 for Bibury. Left after Aldsworth to Coln St. Aldwyns.

Stuart Hodges
Main Street, Coln St Aldwyns,
Cirencester GL7 5AN

Tel	+44 (0)1285 750651
Email	info@thenewinnatcoln.co.uk
Web	www.new-inn.co.uk

The Old School

Comfortable, warm and filled with understated style is this 1854 Cotswold stone house. An easy dining room with a light oak table and chairs doubles as a small board-style meeting room – and Wendy is a grand cook who can whip up a scrumptious working lunch. Afterwards, heaps to do: croquet and boules in the trim garden, a leisurely round of golf nearby, a spin on a quad bike, even falconry. Pile back for another of Wendy's delicious meals then sink into the best room in the house, the upstairs sitting room: a chic, open-plan space with a vaulted ceiling and church style windows that let the light flood in. With squidgy sofas, good art and lovely fabrics it's a super space for intimate celebrations and house parties. For larger groups and weddings a marquee is set up on clipped lawns while live bands play in the orchard – divine! Opt for a hog roast from the local butcher, twirl the night away, then collapse into enormous beds in super-comfy stylish bedrooms. Wendy and John are generous hosts, making this a gorgeous, relaxing place where absolutely nothing is too much trouble. *No civil licence.*

Room hire	1 + marquee: Board (max 12). Cabaret (max 120). Reception (max 120).
Catering	In-house & self-catering.
Sleeps	8 B&B.
Closed	Rarely.
Directions	From Moreton, A44 for Chipping Norton & Oxford. Little Compton 3.5 miles; stay on main road, then right for Chastleton village. House on corner, immed. left into drive.

Wendy Veale & John Scott-Lee
Little Compton, Moreton-in-Marsh GL56 0SL
Tel   +44 (0)1608 674588
Email   wendy@theoldschoolbedandbreakfast.com
Web   www.theoldschoolbedandbreakfast.com

Middle Stanley

Set high on the Cotswold escarpment with glorious views stretching to the Malverns, it's hard to believe this cluster of stone buildings is minutes from the M5. A Victorian farmhouse and outbuildings in 90 green acres offers a flexible setting for business events and celebrations; add a marquee for limitless options. The homely kitchen, grand dining room and lounge hint at creative thinking sessions or relaxing weekend get-togethers; an eclectic mix of bedrooms, all comfortable, are dotted around the complex. The well-equipped Meeting Room (great too for receptions and dinners) is a beautifully refurbished, strikingly furnished barn. A long glass table and jazzy red upholstered chairs set the scene, vibrant paintings adorn pale walls; break-out sessions are held in the Craft Studio. Party the night away in the Latin-influenced Havana Club; it's a refreshment zone for meetings by day. The kitchens are at your disposal, or ask capable Chris about local caterers. Kick back and relax in the cellar games room, with theatre style cinema room, PS3 and Sky; outdoors, fish for trout, play tennis, explore the woods.

Room hire	3 + marquee: Board (max 30). Cabaret (max 160). Theatre (max 45). Reception (max 160).
Catering	Approved caterers.
Sleeps	24: 1 B&B or S/C house for 12: 1 S/C house for 8. 1 S/C studio for 4.
Closed	Never.
Directions	M5 junc. 9, A46, B4077 dir. Stow. Right to Gretton, right for Prescott. Left 300 yds after Stanley P. sign, left by Cotswold stone house.

💰💰💰

Chris Williams
Middle Stanley Farm, Stanley Pontlarge,
Cheltenham GL54 5HE

Tel	+44 (0)1242 673119
Email	cg.williams@live.co.uk
Web	www.middlestanley.co.uk

Upper Court

A splendid Georgian manor in acres of landscaped grounds that has all you'd expect from a big country house. Escape hustle and bustle to marry in style, bring friends for a party or the family for a reunion. Or come for a meeting and some exhilarating team-building – perhaps clay pigeon shooting or horse riding. Marry in the church next door or have a civil ceremony in the elegant drawing room, dotted with antiques and gilt-framed oils and with lovely views from every window; hold the reception in an elegant marquee in the gardens. For private dining that oozes glamour, James Benson, ex Claridge's chef, will whip up something fabulous. For hen do's and bridal parties, beauty therapists can pamper and polish. Outside you have the run of 15 acres, so swim in the heated pool in summer, punt on the lake, indulge in a spot of croquet or tennis. Cottages in the grounds have the same comfortable, country-stylish feel and the Dovecote, a romantic bridal suite for two, overlooks the lake. The Herfords' classic good taste, along with their genuine understanding of what's needed, make for a happy experience.

Room hire	3 + marquee: Board (max 25). Cabaret (max 200). Theatre (max 60). Reception (max 200).
Catering	In-house & own caterers.
Sleeps	34: 6 B&B; 28 S/C.
Closed	Christmas.
Directions	M5 junc. 9, A46 to Teddington Hands; left, follow signs for Kemerton. Left at War Memorial. House directly behind parish church.

Bill & Diana Herford
Kemerton, Tewkesbury GL20 7HY
Tel   +44 (0)1386 725351
Email   herfords@uppercourt.co.uk
Web   www.uppercourt.co.uk

Entry 72   Map 3

The Master Builder's House Hotel

The position is faultless: wide lawns roll down from the the edge of the New Forest village to the Beaulieu river, and a vast sky hangs overhead. This exquisite red-brick house, built in 1729, was home to shipwrights who served the British fleet. Today's interiors mix contemporary stylishness with classical design. A roaring fire, huge sofa, expansive watery views and earthy colours greet you, while gorgeous, colourful bedrooms await upstairs and in the annexe. Flexibility is the key. You can choose the Chichester Room or the pretty teal-coloured Riverview Restaurant for meetings large and small and for celebrations; for intimate wedding receptions out of peak season too – wonderful for a cosy winter wedding. There's even a little private dining room for quieter lunches and dinners. The Master Builder's doesn't do packages; Michael and his team work with you instead to make your event your own, and you can ask for as much or as little help as you like. Whatever you choose, work with the head chef to create your own delicious menu, using local New Forest produce; fish is a speciality. *No civil licence.*

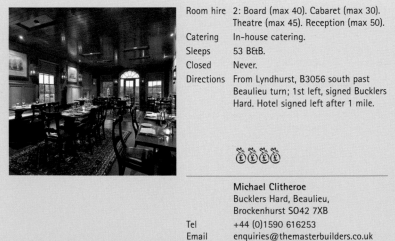

Room hire	2: Board (max 40). Cabaret (max 30). Theatre (max 45). Reception (max 50).
Catering	In-house catering.
Sleeps	53 B&B.
Closed	Never.
Directions	From Lyndhurst, B3056 south past Beaulieu turn; 1st left, signed Bucklers Hard. Hotel signed left after 1 mile.

Michael Clitheroe
Bucklers Hard, Beaulieu,
Brockenhurst SO42 7XB

Tel	+44 (0)1590 616253
Email	enquiries@themasterbuilders.co.uk
Web	www.themasterbuilders.co.uk

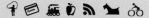

The Tithe Barn

Old Ditcham Farm covers 300 bewitching acres of the South Downs, with tree-covered hills in the distance. Stroll past stately black swans on the pond and down a path edged with delicate, fairylit trees to this imposing 16th-century barn. Massive wooden doors open to a vast and cathedral-like interior: a flagstone floor, a vaulted ceiling, soaring stone arches and half-hammer beams – a stylishly restored space lit by spotlights and warmed by underfloor heating. At one end is a pretty balcony – the former grain bins – where leather sofas open their arms to weary dancers. There's a dressing room for the bride to get ready in, and an industrial kitchen for caterers (Sam and Gaynor, the friendly and efficient managers, will provide a list). Great glass-fronted doors on either side of the barn can be opened up in summer for guests to spill into the lovely meadow. The young – and the young at heart – will want to throw off their shoes and gad about… But this is not just a party place. Conference and exhibition groups would settle in beautifully too, relaxing into the convivial surroundings.

Room hire	1: Cabaret (max 250). Theatre (max 250). Reception (max 250).
Catering	Approved caterers.
Closed	Rarely.
Directions	Directions on booking.

Sam Powers
Old Ditcham Farm,
Petersfield GU31 5RQ

Tel   +44 (0)1730 825562
Email   admin@tithe-barn.co.uk
Web   www.tithe-barn.co.uk

Seafin

She's sleek, elegant and full of character, and moored on the lovely river Hamble, where cormorants dive, woods tumble down to the water's edge and the views are glorious. Built in 1961, the 75ft Seafin has been gutted and beautifully restored by Warwick. Outside, she's white and dashing; inside, she gleams golden with polished wood. The wooden top deck is the place for soaking up the sun, while the picture-windowed aft deck, with big circular table and drop-down screen, acts as dining or board room; down a few steps is a warm, comfortable, book-lined saloon and a chic bar. Charter Seafin for a day and arrive in time for breakfast; sip Pimms as you set off upriver to explore the 18th-century village where Nelson's warships were built. Return for an abundant and appetising lunch provided by onshore caterers, then off to the Isle of Wight to jet ski….. The enthusiastic staff will ensure you have a great day from start to finish. Brilliant for parties or business events or – if you can curtail your guest list – a spectacular setting for a hen or stag bash! *Charters usually between 1 April & 31 October.*

Room hire	Whole yacht: Board (max 12). Reception (max 30).
Catering	In-house, approved & own caterers.
Sleeps	6 B&B.
Closed	December-February.
Directions	Directions on website.

Warwick Bergin
HHF Pontoon, Port Hamble Marina,
Hamble-le-Rice SO31 4QD
Tel +44 (0)20 7264 1020
Email wbergin@trianglepartners.co.uk
Web www.seafin.co.uk

Winforton Court

Dating from 1500, the Court is dignified in its old age – a historic colourful home with undulating floors, great oak beams, thick walls and exceptional timber-framed bedrooms. A walled garden greets you, its path edged with sage studded with perennial geraniums; there are fine views across the Wye Valley to the Black Mountains, and a lovely walk to the river. The sunny courtyard behind has mature trees, cherubs on walls and a tinkling fountain. Beyond, the terraced garden is dominated by a weeping willow, with the sweetest little summer house peeping out from beneath its branches; there are emerald lawns, flower-packed beds, a stream and a small water garden. Come for an intimate wedding, a family celebration – take the whole house for a weekend and a make real party of it – or a meeting. The dramatic saffron-coloured Long Gallery with its striking table glows and sparkles by candlelight; expand the party in the small marquee and gazebo. There's even a private sitting room attached, with comfy sofas for quiet moments. Your hosts are delightful and can advise on local producers and caterers. *No civil licence.*

Room hire	1: Board (max 25). Reception (max 80).
Catering	Approved & own caterers.
Sleeps	6 B&B.
Closed	20-30 December.
Directions	From Hereford, A438 into village. Past Sun Inn, house on left with a green sign & iron gates.

Jackie Kingdon
Winforton HR3 6EA

Tel	+44 (0)1544 328498
Email	jackie@winfortoncourt.co.uk
Web	www.winfortoncourt.co.uk

South Farm

This is no ordinary farm: find acres of safe habitat for birds and animals, angora goats, kune kune pigs, happy hens; relish the taste of super-fresh organic produce, mostly home-grown or reared, gorgeously presented, luscious tasting, paired with fine wines and served with flair. The garden is equally stunning: 15,000 bulbs in the Winter Garden burst into a flame of colour in spring and the Summer Garden hides a sweet summerhouse for wedding vows. The elm-framed Tudor Barn is the largest, most impressive room for a wedding breakfast, while smaller meetings or parties suit the rustic Granary or elegant Drawing Room with its antiquarian books. Alternatively, the Conservatory makes an unusual venue with a showering of lush plants and flowers. Bridal couples are spoiled in a studio and there are several guest bedrooms, plus four romantic Romany caravans and a campsite. For corporate events possibilities are endless: fly fishing, punting, charity auctions, cookery courses… Flexible and unruffled staff give you the freedom to choose, organise and dream. As green as can be, and scrumptious.

Room hire	3: Board (max 16). Cabaret (max 140). Theatre (max 180). Reception (max 250).
Catering	In-house catering.
Sleeps	24 B&B.
Closed	Rarely.
Directions	From Royston, A1198 north for 5 miles, left to Shingay-cum-Wendy. After 2 miles first left to Abington Piggots. House 0.5 miles on right.

Ethical Collection: Environment; Food.
See page 208 for details

James & Philip Paxman
Shingay-cum-Wendy,
Royston SG8 0HR

Tel	+44 (0)1223 207581
Email	james@south-farm.co.uk
Web	www.south-farm.co.uk

The Energy Centre

Along winding lanes, in glorious Wealdean countryside, this converted oast house rests calmly amid acres of orchard, rolls of lawn and organic gardens; birdsong is your soundtrack. Relaxed, intimate, it feels a million miles from hectic city life, yet is only an hour from London. At its centre is a sun-splashed cobble courtyard with a rippling fountain and roses, a magnificent Himalayan palm and a garden treatment centre with an individual menu of therapies. Ian and Shelley left the advertising world behind to create a space where you can simply 'be'. Dedicated, fun-loving, their personal attention is the special ingredient – and Shelley is a fine, thoughtful cook for smaller groups. For informal or alternative wedding receptions (Shelley is a practising shaman), for team-building, life-marking events and tailormade retreats – their speciality – the whole place is yours. Bright uncluttered bedrooms are bejewelled with Asian silks, the conservatory is ideal for meetings and the suite, with a swagged canopy on a vast bed and a bathroom on the mezzanine, has courtyard views. Wonderfully different. *No civil licence.*

Room hire	1+ marquee, tipi, yurt: Board (max 12). Cabaret (max 50). Theatre (max 50). Reception (max 50).
Catering	In-house & own caterers.
Sleeps	8 B&B or S/C.
Closed	Christmas & New Year.
Directions	From M25 junc. 5 A21 to Hastings. Left onto A262 for Goudhurst, then Horsmonden. Follow onto School House Lane, right to School House Oast.

Ian & Shelley Sishton
School House Oast, School House Lane,
Horsmonden, Tonbridge TN12 8BW

Tel	+44 (0)1892 722191
Email	info@the-energy-centre.com
Web	www.the-energy-centre.com

Wallett's Court Country House Hotel & Spa

A fabulous position with sweeping fields heading south towards white cliffs, this country-house hotel is in an AONB: a lovely spot for couples to tie the knot. Dating from 1627 and standing opposite a Norman church, the timber-framed interiors are fresh and up-to-date and have been used for film locations and shoots for *Vogue*. If your wedding party numbers top 180, there are eight acres of grounds with lush lawns – perfect for a marquee – and tennis court and boules; there's quad-biking and clay shooting too for adventurous team-building. The oak-beamed main dining room with crackling fire would make a cosy venue for a winter wedding, and formal parties will love the attached airy conservatory. There's an indoor pool, and relaxing spa treatments in cabins hidden in the trees. Catch the high-speed train from London for an informal meeting in the fabulous tipi, with driftwood floors and reindeer skins ('glamping' is on offer too). Pampering bedrooms are four-poster up a Jacobean staircase or swish contemporary; bathrooms smart. Close to Canterbury cathedral, Dover Castle, a secluded beach… lovely.

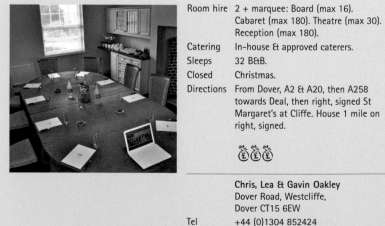

Room hire	2 + marquee: Board (max 16). Cabaret (max 180). Theatre (max 30). Reception (max 180).
Catering	In-house & approved caterers.
Sleeps	32 B&B.
Closed	Christmas.
Directions	From Dover, A2 & A20, then A258 towards Deal, then right, signed St Margaret's at Cliffe. House 1 mile on right, signed.

Chris, Lea & Gavin Oakley
Dover Road, Westcliffe,
Dover CT15 6EW

Tel	+44 (0)1304 852424
Email	stay@thewhitecliffs.com
Web	www.wallettscourt.com

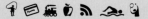

The Pines Calyx

Unique, special and inspiring: this three-year-old building is stunningly gracious and at the cutting edge of ecological design. Find acres of organic gardens, pristine lawns, large spreading trees, a grass labyrinth, a moody bronze of Churchill peering over to nearby France and a floaty lake; all just begging to be photographed. Interiors are awesome: on the first floor, the upper roundel is light, spacious and domed with rammed chalk walls, a crescent roof light and a recovered Japanese Maple floor; spill out from here onto the terrace for wedding drinks. The lower roundel has views across the gardens and lake; both have natural air conditioning for a balanced temperature and the use of a comma-shaped seminar room as a break-out space or for exhibitions. Your party will be fed well: organic vegetables and soft fruit from the kitchen garden, locally sourced meat or fish. Views across the channel are calming, Louise and her staff are wholly reassuring, so even the bride and her mother can feel serene, and you are championing all that is good – without being evangelical – about being green.

Room hire	3: Board (max 40). Cabaret (max 50). Theatre (max 100). Reception (max 100).
Catering	In-house, approved & own caterers.
Closed	Christmas & New Year.
Directions	Go through St Margaret's village. Follow hill down towards beach, through hairpin bend, take next right signed Pines Calyx and Pines Garden.

Louise Kjaertinge
The Pines Garden, Beach Road,
St. Margaret's Bay CT15 6DZ
Tel   +44 (0)1304 851737
Email   louise@pinescalyx.co.uk
Web   www.pinescalyx.co.uk

Ethical Collection: Environment; Community; Food. See page 208 for details

Quenby Hall

Past grazing longhorn cattle, through ancient woodland, over a stone bridge, lies a Jacobean gem. Beautifully restored to their 17th-century prime, ornate plaster ceilings and glowing wood panelling grace this stately family home 20 minutes from Leicester. Two rooms are licensed for weddings: the Great Hall, dominated by a huge fireplace, fossil-studded marble floors and suits of armour; and the elegant Brown Parlour, its oak-panelled walls hung with portraits and ornate mirrors. All are suited to business meetings and conferences too, while smaller gatherings have the Library, a haven of Persian rugs and squashy sofas. A grand oak staircase leads to the magnificent ballroom, a sophisticated setting for soirées. The pretty walled garden is a favourite with wedding photographers; pitch your marquee on the cedar-fringed lawn behind the house, or party in the rustic stone-flagged Dairy, complete with bar. Owner Aubyn and events manager Sarah are meticulous planners and can arrange country pursuits of every ilk. Trusted caterers cover everything from intimate meals in the Hall to banquets in the marquee.

Room hire	4 + marquee: Board (max 20). Cabaret (max 250). Theatre (max 100). Reception (max 250)
Catering	Approved caterers.
Closed	Christmas & New Year.
Directions	Directions on website.

Aubyn de Lisle
Hungarton LE7 9JF

Tel	+44 (0)116 259 5224
Email	enquiries@quenbyhall.co.uk
Web	www.quenbyhall.co.uk

Washingborough Hall

A pretty 18th-century limestone manor house next to the village church, surrounded by lawns, mature beech and yew trees. Friendly Lucy and Edward are restoring the house to the peak of its Georgian splendour; Messrs Farrow & Ball are well-represented. With outdoor pursuits on tap in the Lincolnshire countryside, house parties and corporate get-togethers are well catered for here; after a day in the fresh air, the house is a welcoming place to relax and unwind. Either side of the comfortable hall are the large, impressive dining and Sibthorpe rooms, both flooded with light from huge bay windows. Small conferences and wedding ceremonies take place in the stately elegance of Sibthorpe, while the dining room, with an original Adam fireplace, is just right for a board meeting or formal celebratory meal; the chef is an imaginative advocate of seasonal British food. The cosy bar and snug, with requisite country prints and cartoons, are great places to kick back or hold small informal meetings. Bedrooms and bathrooms are undergoing renovation, making the most of fine antique furniture and original fireplaces.

Room hire	5: Board (max 24). Cabaret (max 50). Theatre (max 35). Reception (max 100).
Catering	In-house catering.
Sleeps	24 B&B.
Closed	Rarely.
Directions	From Lincoln City east 2.5 miles on B1190, enter village, at mini r'bout turn right up Church Hill, Washingborough Hall up hill on left.

Lucy & Edward Herring
Church Hill, Washingborough LN4 1BE
Tel   +44 (0)1522 790340
Email   enquiries@washingboroughhall.com
Web   www.washingboroughhall.com

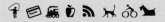

Entry 82   Map 6

The Isla Gladstone Conservatory

Exclusively yours! A spectacular space for the really big occasion: the ethereal splendour of a vast Victorian glasshouse. Set in a 100-acre park, this confection of delicately wrought white metal and glass has been magnificently restored and brought into the 21st century with a climate-controlled interior and the last word in high-tech facilities. Underneath is a bistro (also available, but evenings only) where the glass is engraved with designs by Isla Gladstone herself, an Arts & Crafts artist who married into the prime-ministerial family. Local lass Gemma is in charge of everything. Her enthusiasm for the place and its possibilities – from weddings and conferences to film shoots – is boundless and she's immensely proud of her staff and the food: fresh, locally sourced and cooked on the premises. Bride and groom can make their vows in the fairytale expanses of the conservatory or in the open air, under the pretty bandstand. There's a room for the bride to change in, too, and in the evening guests have Stanley Park all to themselves to wander, glass in hand, among the rose walks and stone pavilions.

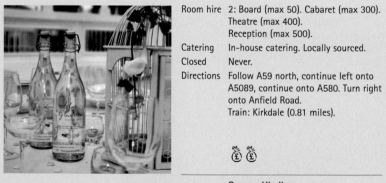

Room hire	2: Board (max 50). Cabaret (max 300). Theatre (max 400). Reception (max 500).
Catering	In-house catering. Locally sourced.
Closed	Never.
Directions	Follow A59 north, continue left onto A5089, continue onto A580. Turn right onto Anfield Road. Train: Kirkdale (0.81 miles).

Gemma Hindley
Stanley Park, Liverpool L4 0TD

Tel   +44 (0)151 263 0363
Email   info@theislagladstone.co.uk
Web   www.theislagladstone.co.uk

October Gallery

Strikingly unusual – a gallery that is colourful, convivial and professional too. Director Chilli Hawes leads the team serenely and runs the sort of place that takes in dancing dervishes, Balinese and Indian dance troupes, poets, writers and artists from the transcultural avant-garde. This is a gallery of ideas, and often of very beautiful art works. We loved it when we launched a book here; the various spaces lend themselves seamlessly to parties, meetings and conferences; rehearsals and exhibitions too. The building seethes with interest: there is a big L-shaped downstairs gallery space and a charming courtyard, with fruit trees, shrubs and flowers – lovely on balmy evenings. Ask about availability of the bright and airy theatre space upstairs, complete with Bechstein piano, excellent acoustics and professional sound system. Upstairs again is the spacious Club Room, whose leather armchairs and sofas, book-lined walls and board room tables are what one might expect from the Atheneaum or Travellers' Club. No port, no cigars, but everything else. It is delightful, informal and surprising.

Room hire	3: Board (max 10). Cabaret (max 21). Theatre (max 80). Reception (max 120).
Catering	Approved & own caterers.
Closed	Every Sunday. August.
Directions	Gallery off Queens Square. Buses to Southhampton Row: 168, 68, 59, 91. Tube: Holborn, Russell Square. Mainline Rail: Euston.

24 Old Gloucester Street,
Bloomsbury, London WC1N 3AL

Tel	+44 (0)20 7242 7367
Email	rentals@octobergallery.co.uk
Web	www.octobergallery.co.uk

Friends House

First impressions count, and the grand colonnaded entrance to the Friends House cuts a dash on the busy Euston Road. You enter from a quiet garden to one side, then climb a splendid marble staircase to an imposing landing. There are a myriad of sober and airy rooms for medium-sized meetings and training sessions; and then there's the Large Hall, a vast, grand space with a gallery and excellent acoustics that seats 1,100 theatre-style. Smaller conferences are held in the Small Hall, elegant and serene with beautiful circular windows. The four-room Garden Suite is perfect for small private meetings and interviews. You have all the gadgetry you could want, with WiFi, projectors, blackout blinds, video conferencing, even a piano which you can play. The day delegate rate includes in-room catering, or you can head to the Bookshop Café for a light lunch or snack (fairtrade, vegetarian, much organic) or down to the restaurant for a fuller meal; receptions – non-alcoholic – are in the pretty courtyard garden. Quaker ethical and environmental standards set the tone – matched by simplicity and value for money. *No alcohol.*

Room hire	22: Board (max 48). Cabaret (max 48). Theatre (max 1,100).
Catering	In-house catering.
Closed	Rarely.
Directions	From Euston Station, cross over Euston Rd. From Euston Square right out of station, then right to Euston Rd. Disabled parking in Endsleigh Gardens.

Ethical Collection: Environment; Food.
See page 208 for details

Paul Grey
Friends House, 173 Euston Road,
London NW1 2BJ

Tel	+44 (0)20 7663 1094
Email	events@quaker.org.uk
Web	www.friendshouse.co.uk

Entry 85   Map 3

MIC Hotel & Conference Centre

It's central London, but you'd scarcely believe it from the quiet side-street entrance and handsome façade of Euston House, home of the MIC. This social enterprise centre offers the full works for conferences and meetings plus dining and sleeping, at affordable rates and with style. A smart entrance hall leads down to the light-filled, zingy Atrium café bar and restaurant, good for meeting breaks, breakfasts, evening drinks or more formal receptions and conference meals. Menus are refreshingly imaginative, ingredients sourced with care. Flexibility and functionality are the key concepts here, with a range of meeting rooms seating two to 120 and a variety of AV and conferencing facilities (refurbishment is planned for some rooms). Upstairs rooms enjoy natural light, good ventilation and opening windows, while the largest, at sub-ground level, is illuminated by a huge skylight. For those who need to stay, there are also smart and comfortable bedrooms. Great value, highly professional and friendly service, coupled with attractive public spaces – you'd be hard pressed to find a better deal in this part of London.

Room hire	15: Board (max 50). Cabaret (max 100). Theatre (max 120). Reception (max 150).
Catering	In-house, approved & own caterers.
Sleeps	58 B&B.
Closed	Never.
Directions	From Euston Square tube, head along North Gower St. 2nd right at Euston St. From Euston station 3-minute walk along Euston St.

James Barr
81–103 Euston Street,
London NW1 2EZ

Tel	+44 (0)20 7380 0001
Email	sales@micentre.com
Web	www.micentre.com

The Troubadour

Bob Dylan played here in the 1960s, so did Jimi Hendrix, Joni Mitchell, Paul Simon and the Stones. The Troubadour is a slice of old London cool, a quirky coffee house/bar in Earl's Court with a magical garden, spacious Gallery and funky basement Club – just the place to throw an unforgettable party. Bring your favourite band or DJ (or lovely staff can point you towards a sufficiently cool musician) and whoop it up till late. The white-walled, light-filled Gallery hosts art exhibitions and wine tasting; background music and fresh flowers transform this space for drinks, receptions and dinner parties. They'll serve anything from stylish canapés to hearty veggie meals, from salads to sumptuous evening dinners. Sneak off to the cosy wood-panelled Shackleton room for hen do's or small meetings. The graceful café bar with rows of teapots elegantly displayed in the windows dates from 1954 and the ceiling drips with musical instruments. Next door, two floors above the Gallery, is the Garret. Tip-toe up to this vibrant apartment suite in the eaves: it's got fabulous views over London's rooftops. *No civil licence.*

Room hire	4: Board (max 32). Cabaret (max 50). Theatre (max 60). Reception (max 120).
Catering	In-house catering.
Sleeps	4 B&B.
Closed	Christmas Day, Boxing Day & New Year's Day.
Directions	Tube: Earl's Court or West Brompton (both 5-minute walk). Bus: 74, 328, 430, C1, C3. Car parks £35 a day.

💰💰

Simon & Susie Thornhill
263-267 Old Brompton Road, Earl's Court, London SW5 9JA

Tel	+44 (0)20 7370 1434
Email	susie@troubadour.co.uk
Web	www.troubadour.co.uk

Topolski Century

Almost hidden under the arches of Hungerford Bridge on the South Bank is Feliks Topolski's former workshop, transformed into a modern gallery and funky events space. The artist's works vividly chronicle history's foremost events from World War II to the Swinging 60s and beyond, providing a fabulous focus for a wedding party, celebration or corporate reception. The gallery curves organically through the Century Arches, a 600ft-long painting which snakes its bold, colourful way along the arches, with clever spaces along the way in which guests can mingle and engage more closely with the art. The sleek Chronicle Arch houses a striking series of satirical drawings of 20th-century figures, perfect for small lectures or receptions for up to 50. When the gallery closes to the public you can have it all to yourselves; guests spread out through the curving spaces, mingling freely or clustering for a speech or buffet in the gallery's wider final section, which holds up to 200. Fiona will point you to caterers and make sure your event is super-smooth. It's as smart as can be: a memorable events space.

Room hire	2: Board (max 20). Theatre (max 40). Reception (max 200).
Catering	Approved caterers.
Closed	Christmas Day, Boxing Day, New Year's Eve & Day.
Directions	Next to Royal Festival Hall, South Bank. Tube: Waterloo, Embankment, Westminster. Mainline stations: Waterloo, Charing Cross.

Simon Marshall
150–152 Hungerford Arches,
Concert Hall Approach,
Waterloo, London SE1 8XU

Tel	+44 (0)20 7620 1275
Email	events@topolskicentury.org.uk
Web	www.topolskicentury.org.uk

Siobhan Davies Studios

Energy and movement radiate from this dynamic dance studio in the very thick of central London, just behind the South Bank. The late 19th-century building has been shot through with striking contemporary additions; suspended steel staircases, sprung floors, and a clever fusion of brick, glass, brushed steel and wood give the place a wonderfully airy, uncluttered feel. Run by one of the UK's leading independent dance companies, Siobhan Davies Dance, the studios hold classes during the week, but at weekends you can have the place to yourself for an arty wedding or celebration. Meetings or rehearsals can take place at almost any time. The Roof Studio is the largest, lightest and brightest space, with a high undulating ribbon roof, a lighting rig and black-out blinds (great for a film shoot or performance) but all rooms and landings can be dressed up or down as you wish, a blank canvas for your creativity. Bright outgoing staff help at every stage of the planning and you have oodles of space. This is an RIBA award-winning contemporary arts building with bags of surprises and style. *No civil licence.*

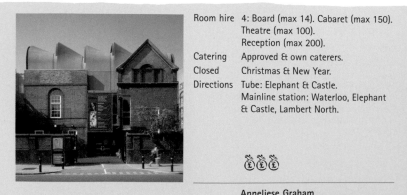

Room hire	4: Board (max 14). Cabaret (max 150). Theatre (max 100). Reception (max 200).
Catering	Approved & own caterers.
Closed	Christmas & New Year.
Directions	Tube: Elephant & Castle. Mainline station: Waterloo, Elephant & Castle, Lambert North.

Anneliese Graham
85 St George's Road, London SE1 6ER

Tel	+44 (0)20 7091 9650
Email	info@siobhandavies.com
Web	www.siobhandavies.com

Cley Windmill

The setting is magical. Rushes flutter in the salt marsh, raised paths lead off to the sea and a vast sky appears to start at your feet. The Windmill is an unusual, authentic and welcoming venue for birthday parties, anniversaries, workshops and small weddings. The round bedrooms in the tower are impossibly romantic for honeymooners, and get smaller as you rise (one is for mountaineers only); you're in the middle of a bird sanctuary so the galleries provide stunning views. There are six rooms in the windmill for your party; combined with the self-catering cottage, the whole place can sleep 20. Imagine the loveliest drawing room – low ceiling, wood-burner, honesty bar, stripped floors… and the prettiest window seat; bedrooms have checked throws, painted furniture and colourful walls. Buffet suppers, formal dinners, canapés, cream teas, Christmassy mulled wine – all this and more can be provided by resident chefs in the beamed and candlelit dining room. The Windmill has a full wedding licence and the jetty onto the creek makes a spectacular spot for your photos – as does the top balcony. *No marquees.*

Room hire	2: Board (max 20). Theatre (max 20).
Catering	In-house catering. Locally sourced.
Sleeps	20: 16 B&B; 4 S/C.
Closed	Never.
Directions	Head east through Cley on A149. Mill signed on left in village.

Charlotte Martin
The Quay, Cley, Holt NR25 7RP

Tel	+44 (0)1263 740209
Email	info@cleywindmill.co.uk
Web	www.cleywindmill.co.uk

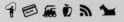

Chaucer Barn

Enter this beautiful Norfolk barn, and gasp – at an elegant and intimate retreat with a difference. Set on a farm once owned by Geoffrey Chaucer, no less, the interior is a fantastic mix of modern, quirky and luxurious: oriental rugs, Indian teak furniture and electric pink and orange sofas, with curtains to match. The cathedral-like kitchen has a minstrel's gallery and a huge table for dining and meeting, and there are break-out spaces galore – flow through into the morning room, or kick your shoes off in the sitting room and the snug upstairs. The stunning games room-cum-sitting area opens onto the patio for summer receptions; for parties, spread out and use the whole house. Unwind at the end of the day in big uncluttered bedrooms with great beds, bold fabrics, super bathrooms. Owners James and Debbie have thought of everything, from a huge flat-screen TV for business presentations to outdoor games and a covered barbecue area for relaxation – in five acres of lovely gardens with endless views. The position is outstanding: the Norfolk Broads are a 20-minute drive, the celebrated coastline is three miles.

Room hire	2: Board (max 18). Cabaret (max 20). Theatre (max 40). Reception (max 100).
Catering	Approved & own caterers.
Sleeps	18 S/C.
Closed	Never.
Directions	From Holt A148 east to Bodham. 1st right, signed 'Gresham'. Follow 3 miles, Chaucer Barn on left.

Debbie Gray
Gresham NR11 8RL

Tel	+44 (0)1263 577733
Email	info@chaucerbarn.com
Web	www.chaucerbarn.com

Barsham Barns

Coming from the city this is nothing short of heaven. Potter Jenny and her architect husband have transformed a complex of brick and flint barns in a pretty valley that is more Cotswolds than Norfolk -- yet the glorious North Coast is five miles away. So you have the best of country-everything including the barns: an enticing palate of flint, cobbles, chalk and beams, warm textures and sophisticated furnishings and, on your doorstep, romantic country sounds – wagtails and warblers, cockerel and sheep. Wedding receptions (marquees are possible), relaxed board meetings and informal training sessions or workshops; cookery courses with a chef, riding, sailing, surfing and fishing can all be organised, while the less adventurous can laze in the jacuzzi, try a yoga course, enjoy beauty treatments or steam themselves happy. Perfect for large family reunions or groups of friends; the kitchens have everything a cook could want and if you're feeling lazy you can even have food delivered. Each barn has its own pretty garden from which footpaths lead to meadows and a view to a little church. Bucolic bliss. *No civil licence.*

Room hire	3 + marquee: Board (max 22). Cabaret (max 120). Reception (max 120).
Catering	Approved & self-catering. Locally sourced.
Sleeps	48 S/C.
Closed	Never.
Directions	A148 Fakenham bypass. Signs to B1105 to Wells-next-the-Sea. After 1 mile, right to the Barshams. Barns on green 1 mile from turning.

💷💷💷

Jenny Dale
Greenway, North Barsham NR22 6AP

Tel	+44 (0)1328 821744
Email	info@barshambarns.co.uk
Web	www.barshambarns.co.uk

Elms Barn

A timeless country wedding on a country estate in South Norfolk: rolling lawns, rose bowers, wooden bridge – even a moat. And a stageset-perfect brick and timbered 17th-century barn. Almost stealing the show from the bride, with its softly glowing brick and aged beams and rafters, the barn can be magically transformed from ceremonial space to dining space while guests chink glasses in the next-door marquee. Spin out the jollities for a few days and stay in the estate's brick-and-beamed cottages, and another converted barn (with elegant bridal suite), all stylishly tricked out in a comfy cottagey way. The in-house chef (nothing is done by halves) can rustle up barbecues and brunches, as well as canapés and banquets for the main event, while guests play croquet or wander the gorgeous gardens. The effortlessly efficient and thoughtful Freelands love sharing their family estate and can organise everything, from the table plan to the Bentley escorting the bride to the barn. You're in safe hands for a stunning day. *Note no weddings over the festive season, but available for meetings, receptions and house parties.*

Room hire	1+ marquee: Cabaret (max 130). Theatre (max 130). Reception (max 175).
Catering	In-house catering.
Sleeps	36: 16 B&B; S/C cottages for 20.
Closed	Christmas, New Year & Easter.
Directions	From Norwich, A146 to Lowestoft. At Gillingham A143 to Great Yarmouth; follow signs to Elms Barn.

Richard & Teena Freeland
The Elms, Toft Monks, Beccles NR34 0EJ

Tel	+44 (0)1502 677380
Email	enquiries@elmsbarnweddings.co.uk
Web	www.elmsbarnweddings.co.uk

Battlesteads Hotel

In the land of castles, stone circles and fortified towers is Battlesteads, an old inn given a fresh lease of life by owners who aim to go as 'green' as possible. The boiler burns wood chips from local sustainable forestry, a polytunnel produces the salads, a tank collects rainwater – greenies can be happy here, so too those searching for a laid-back, warm and delightful venue for weddings, parties and celebrations. Enter a large, cosy, low-beamed and panelled bar with a wood-burning stove; a step further and you find a sunny conservatory dining room (licensed for civil ceremonies) that reaches into a pretty walled garden; spill out here, drink in hand, for photos and a natter. A spacious dining area comes with leather chairs at dark wood tables and kind Dee will fill it with fresh flowers. Menus show a commitment to sourcing locally and the food bursts with flavour; choose a sit-down affair, a buffet or a barbecue – all are equally scrummy. Bridal couples can plump for the spacious, carpeted and comfortable Chipchase Room while there are heaps more spotless bedrooms for all your loved ones.

Room hire	2: Cabaret (max 50). Theatre (max 60). Reception (max 110).
Catering	In-house catering. Locally sourced.
Sleeps	34 B&B.
Closed	3 weeks in February.
Directions	From A69 at Hexham, A6079 to Chollerford, then A6320 for Bellingham; Wark is halfway.

Richard & Dee Slade
Wark, Hexham NE48 3LS

Tel	+44 (0)1434 230209
Email	info@battlesteads.com
Web	www.battlesteads.com

Ethical Collection: Environment; Food.
See page 208 for details

Saughy Rigg Farm

In deepest Northumberland, where the Romans built their forts and famous wall, Saughy Rigg sits proudly in National Trust land. A sympathetically restored 18th-century farmhouse with a pond and resident wildlife by its entrance, it is neat, tidy and inviting inside. The sitting room has a wood-burner to warm weary walkers' toes, and the spacious dining room leads to a well-stocked bar. Wood abounds, and warm, traditionally furnished bedrooms continue the clean and simple theme. In winter, house-party guests can rustle up warming feasts in the large kitchen, and at any time of the year an in-house chef can prepare locally sourced meals – for a celebratory party, a meeting large or small, or an intimate wedding reception. A great spot too for civilised hen-parties! Opportunities for adventuring abound: ramblers will be spoilt for choice, while business teams will bond over orienteering, fishing, even archery. Kath's relaxed and relaxing approach, and her passion for all things eco, inspires the whole place. Breathe deeply, kick off your shoes, you'll feel at home. And don't forget the walking togs.

Room hire	4: Board (max 20). Cabaret (max 50). Theatre (max 30). Reception (max 70).
Catering	In-house catering.
Sleeps	25 B&B or S/C.
Closed	Never.
Directions	Directions on website.

Kath Doule
Twice Brewed, Haltwhistle NE49 9PT

Tel	+44 (0)1434 344120
Email	info@saughyrigg.co.uk
Web	www.saughyrigg.co.uk

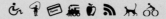

Hodsock Priory & Courtyard

An imposing Tudor gatehouse, one of only five in the country, sets the scene. This 19th-century Nottinghamshire house was built to look like a proper red brick Tudor pile, with mullioned windows and decorative chimneys. Its setting couldn't be better; five acres of beautifully laid out grounds – plenty of room for a marquee – include a lake, river, formal Italian gardens, terraces, rare trees and millions of snowdrops in February – a photographer's dream. George, Katharine, and efficient manager Lynda are always on hand to help with arrangements for weddings, celebrations and meetings. Marriage ceremonies and drinks receptions are held in the grand oak-panelled hall; guests gather in the chandeliered anteroom for smaller parties, and may retreat to the quiet comfort of the book-lined library. The light and airy bar combines ornate plasterwork, dark oak floors and a marble fireplace with a relaxed, contemporary feel. It leads to the brand new Pavilion; a large square room with cream walls and French windows onto the terrace. Upstairs are three top-notch suites, and ten brand new rooms in the grounds for guests.

Room hire	4 + courtyard & marquee: Board (max 24). Cabaret (max 120). Theatre (max 200). Reception (max 250).
Catering	Approved & own caterers.
Sleeps	26 B&B or 6 B&B & 20 S/C.
Closed	Please check with owner.
Directions	Leave Worksop on Blyth Road (B6045). Past Bassetlaw Hospital, cont. 3.5 miles. Through double bend, over small river. Left to Priory.

💰💰💰

George & Katharine Buchanan
Hodsock, Worksop S81 0TY

Tel	+44 (0)1909 591204
Email	gb@hodsockpriory.com
Web	www.hodsockpriory.com

Forever Green

Cocooned in a clearing amidst conifers and native deciduous trees. This striking, triple-height, contemporary steel and glass structure stands in thick woodland on a 70-acre ex-hospital site on the outskirts of Mansfield. Hobnob in clean-lined, leaf-hued interiors flooded with light, as the bring-the-outside-in windows provide a towering natural vista with an informal feel from the recently renovated and comfort-cooled interior. Whether it's an exclusive-use wedding, a rah-rah team-building day run by local specialists or a corporate do, erstwhile well-respected restaurateur/manager Paul is keen to offer a personal experience. Enjoy deliciously fresh food produced by the in-house team, sourced from their own orchards and herb gardens; free-range eggs come from down the road, the rest from local shire suppliers. Big greenie points abound: animal and bird rescue organisations release their charges into the thickets already populated with fox, deer and woodpecker. And if your numbers top 150, ask about a marquee (for up to 700) – there's oodles of space amongst the wild flowers and woodland walks.

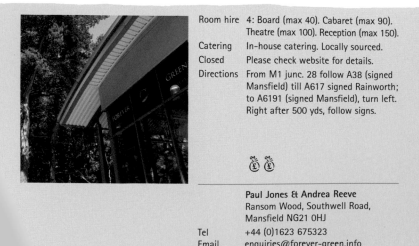

Room hire	4: Board (max 40). Cabaret (max 90). Theatre (max 100). Reception (max 150).
Catering	In-house catering. Locally sourced.
Closed	Please check website for details.
Directions	From M1 junc. 28 follow A38 (signed Mansfield) till A617 signed Rainworth; to A6191 (signed Mansfield), turn left. Right after 500 yds, follow signs.

Paul Jones & Andrea Reeve
Ransom Wood, Southwell Road,
Mansfield NG21 0HJ

Tel	+44 (0)1623 675323
Email	enquiries@forever-green.info
Web	www.forever-green.info

Langar Hall

Langar Hall is a most engaging and delightful place. Imogen's exquisite style and natural joie de vivre make this a mecca for those in search of a warm, country-house atmosphere for an intimate wedding, a celebratory bash or a private meeting. The house sits atop a barely noticeable hill in glorious parkland, bang next door to the 12-century village church – couples can wander over for a blessing after a civil ceremony in the dramatic, pillared dining room. Imo's family came here over 150 years ago; much of what fills the house arrived then, and it's easy to feel intoxicated by beautiful things: statues and busts, ancient tomes in overflowing bookshelves, a good collection of oil paintings. Wedding breakfasts are always three heavenly courses, simply prepared, so come for Langar lamb, fish from Brixham or game from Belvoir Castle. Later spill onto the terrace to wrap up your evening with a spectacular firework display. Bedrooms are wonderful, some resplendent with antiques, others with fabrics draped from beams or trompe l'œil panelling. In the grounds is an adorable chalet, just for two. Idyllic.

Room hire	4 + marquee: Board (max 14). Cabaret (max 120). Reception (max 120).
Catering	In-house catering.
Sleeps	24 B&B.
Closed	Never.
Directions	From Nottingham, A52 towards Grantham. Right, signed Cropwell Bishop, then straight on for 5 miles. House next to church on edge of village, signed.

Imogen Skirving
Church Lane, Langar,
Nottingham NG13 9HG

Tel	+44 (0)1949 860559
Email	info@langarhall.co.uk
Web	www.langarhall.com

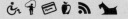

Miller of Mansfield

This handsome coaching inn sits proudly on the high street, a timeless model of Edwardian splendour – or so it seems. Inside, worlds gently collide, with 18th-century exteriors giving way to 21st-century fixtures and fittings. You'll find sand-blasted beams, black suede stools, silver-leaf wallpaper above open fires, fairylight chandeliers dangling from the ceilings. The tantalising Velvet Room seats 14 for a meeting or private dinner, and there's seriously good food, from working lunches to six-course affairs. The airy restaurant doubles as a conference space, all facilities laid on. Team-building activities include clay-shooting and gliding down the Thames in electric launches. For a wedding reception with more than a touch of glamour, marry in one of the many nearby Norman churches (one just across the Green) and, as the bells peal, stroll back for a champagne reception on the terrace. Bigger groups can spill into a marquee on the terraced gardens. Upstairs, bedrooms are lively; the chrome four-poster has a leather headboard. Definitely one for the young at heart. *Min. stay two nights at weekends.*

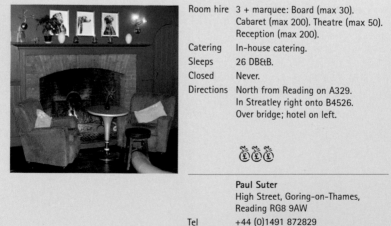

Room hire	3 + marquee: Board (max 30). Cabaret (max 200). Theatre (max 50). Reception (max 200).
Catering	In-house catering.
Sleeps	26 DB&B.
Closed	Never.
Directions	North from Reading on A329. In Streatley right onto B4526. Over bridge; hotel on left.

Paul Suter
High Street, Goring-on-Thames,
Reading RG8 9AW

Tel	+44 (0)1491 872829
Email	reservations@millerofmansfield.com
Web	www.millerofmansfield.com

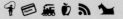

Kingston Bagpuize House

A delightful 17th-century pocket-size stately home, in stunning grounds at the end of a country lane... when you first catch sight of it you may think all that's missing is a Jane Austen heroine to pluck the roses. Four charming, elegant, high-ceilinged rooms are yours for the day, to use as you please. The bright drawing room and entrance hall with its magnificent cantilevered staircase are licensed for civil ceremonies; with the library and dining room, they make enchanting spaces for wedding breakfasts and celebrations; play Lord and Lady of the Manor for the day. Virginia has decorated this very romantic house with grace and flair, so that it feels inviting and welcoming in spite of the grandeur: the impeccable period furniture, the fine porcelain, the subtle touches of chinoiserie and Delft. A list of approved caterers helps you get the dining right; they can have the run of the kitchen, or can work from a marquee on the lawn. Afterwards guests can wander the magnificent gardens, a classic English combination of herbaceous and shrub borders, woodland, parkland and flawless lawns.

Room hire	4 + marquee: Board (max 14). Cabaret (max 300). Theatre (max 60). Reception (max 500).
Catering	Approved caterers.
Closed	Rarely.
Directions	From Abingdon A415 to Kingston Bagpuize. Access via Rectory Lane (on left after 30mph sign). Right into driveway, under archway, house on right.

💰💰💰

Virginia Grant
Kingston Bagpuize, Abingdon OX13 5AX

Tel	+44 (0)1865 820259
Email	info@kingstonbagpuizehouse.org.uk
Web	www.kingstonbagpuizehouse.org.uk

Old Bank Hotel

A hugely convenient place for conferences, board meetings, private lunches and dinners and intimate wedding breakfasts; this is the heart of old Oxford. Stroll south past Corpus Christi to Christ Church meadows, head north for All Souls, the Radcliffe Camera and the Bodleian Library. Inside find warm contemporary elegance with an important collection of modern art and photography adorning most walls; guests receive an art catalogue when checking in. The Gallery has natural lighting and a stunning Damien Hirst piece, but you have all the high-tech gadgetry and facilities needed for high-level presentations and gatherings. The Board Room is oak panelled and has a large skylight; private dining in both rooms will be delicious (fish from the Channel Islands, meat from the owner's farm). Service is serene and the old tiller's hall is now a vibrant bar/brasserie with fine arched windows – perfect for chilling out after a hard day working. If you choose to stay, bedrooms are gorgeous with super bathrooms, big comfy beds and all the audio-visual wizardry you could want. Bigger rooms have sofas, *Off-street parking included. No civil licence.*

Room hire	4: Board (max 30). Cabaret (max 24). Theatre (max 50). Reception (max 70).
Catering	In-house catering.
Sleeps	81 B&B.
Closed	Never.
Directions	Cross Magdalen Bridge for city centre. Straight through 1st set of lights, then left into Merton St. Follow road right; 1st right into Magpie Lane. Car park 2nd right.

£££

Ben Truesdale
92-94 High Street, Oxford OX1 4BN

Tel	+44 (0)1865 799599
Email	info@oldbank-hotel.co.uk
Web	www.oldbank-hotel.co.uk

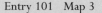

Old Parsonage Hotel

Have you set your heart on a city wedding but with a country-house feel? Come here. This is a delightful and intimate place for a small, relaxed party, and the Pike Room, with its Russian red walls and crackling fire, is licensed for civil ceremonies. It can seat 16 for delicious meals (fish from the Channel Islands, meat from the owner's farm, as at its sister hotel, the Old Bank) and is also the place for business meetings with a convivial vibe and all the equipment you need; private dining can be arranged here, too. Plenty of space and lovely places to escape abound: a buzzing bar for a glass of champagne and live jazz, a rooftop terrace for afternoon tea, a hidden garden where you can sit and listen to the bells of St Giles, and an extensive art collection to admire. Warm stylish bedrooms with superbly comfortable beds and marble bathrooms are scattered all over the place. Daily walking tours led by a resident art expert are 'on the house', the staff are the best, and the hotel will book you a punt on the Cherwell and even pack a picnic: how romantic for lovers to glide effortlessly through meadows and spires.

Room hire	1: Board (max 16). Cabaret (max 16). Reception (max 20).
Catering	In-house catering.
Sleeps	63 B&B.
Closed	Never.
Directions	From A40 ring road, south onto Banbury Road thro' Summertown. Hotel on right just before St Giles Church.

Deniz Bostanci
1 Banbury Road, Oxford OX2 6NN

Tel	+44 (0)1865 310210
Email	info@oldparsonage-hotel.co.uk
Web	www.oldparsonage-hotel.co.uk

Caswell House

A handsome 15th-century manor house with an ancient orchard, walled gardens, smooth lawns and a moat brimming with trout. Bride, groom and wedding guests can sashay over an arched bridge and into a marquee. How splendid is that? Amanda and Richard are generous and easy-going and their three stone and slate barns, with 12-foot thick walls, massive beams and flagged floors, will entertain up to 200 guests and are licensed to hold civil ceremonies; add a marquee if you need to increase your numbers further. They can advise on local organic caterers and the feast can be served in the marquee or Wenmans Barn. The house has a flagstoned hall leading to a sitting room with vast fireplaces and squishy sofas. Comfortable bedrooms have shower rooms and gorgeous views of the garden. The newly weds will love the snug rustic Coach House with its honey-coloured stonework and rich colours; there are two more immaculately renovated retreats so all is perfect for families gathering and friends celebrating luxurious country living. Delicious Aga breakfasts, snooker and plenty of rolling acres to ramble: lovely.

Room hire	4 + marquee: Board (max 30). Cabaret (max 200). Theatre (max 200). Reception (max 500).
Catering	Approved caterers.
Sleeps	12: 6 B&B; 6 S/C.
Closed	Rarely.
Directions	A40 Burford to Oxford. Right after 1.8 miles dir. Brize Norton, left at staggered x-roads. Right then left at r'bouts; on for 1.2 miles, house on right.

£££

Kate Matthews
Caswell Lane, Brize Norton OX18 3NJ

Tel	+44 (0)1993 701064
Email	weddings@caswell-house.co.uk
Web	www.caswell-house.co.uk

Map 3

The Tythe Barn

The separate bits are super, but put them together and they add up to even more than the sum of their parts. The barn itself is a glorious, thatched stone building, 100ft-long and over 600 years old. Inside, golden walls, arching beams and huge glass doors give an awe-inspiring, almost ecclesiastical feel. Whether you're married here or elsewhere (perhaps in the 12th-century church next door?) it's a stunning setting for a wedding breakfast. Or for a party, seminar or conference; all is laid on. (If your numbers top 220, ask about a marquee.) Raymond Blanc brings his staff here for Christmas parties, so the food must be pretty top-notch... The adjoining Cowshed (available as an alternative venue but not if the barn is in use) and newly planted garden with elegant seating provide quiet retreats, while one wing of the Manor House has a charming bridal suite. Don't forget, you're on a family-owned working farm and if the drive from the unlovely ring road is somewhat underwhelming, don't be put off. This is an imaginative and delightful venue, and the affable Deeleys devote themselves to the pursuit of perfection.

Room hire	2: Board (max 46). Cabaret (max 80). Theatre (max 180). Reception (max 220).
Catering	In-house catering.
Sleeps	7 B&B.
Closed	Rarely.
Directions	5-minute drive from junc. 9, M40. Directions on website.

Emma Deeley
Manor Farm, Launton OX26 5DP

Tel	+44 (0)1869 321442
Email	info@thetythebarn.co.uk
Web	www.thetythebarn.co.uk

Zanzibarn

Weave your way down country lanes to this beautifully restored threshing barn. Chickens fuss, horses ruminate and a peacock surveys the scene. Wildlife is on show inside, too: discover antique zebra hides and a splendid collection of East African hunting trophies. The theme continues, with more hides draped on bannisters and a spectacular antler chandelier between the beams. The space is vast, all warm wood, Asian rugs, flowers and candles, and a long dining table prettily set for dinner guests. A great place for a celebration, Zanzibarn includes an Indian-style area upstairs with sofas, throws and wall hangings; survey the dancing from the balcony. Huge windows on both floors make the most of daylight, while nights are made magical by two wood-burners and numerous tea lights sparkling in alcoves. Owners Emma and Charlie live next door, and have a list of caterers, a separate-access kitchen and advice for events planners. There's a tennis court for the sporty, and great walking from the door. A dash of East Africa in softly rolling Shropshire: this will be a party to remember!

Room hire 1: Board (max 45). Cabaret (max 70). Reception (max 100).
Catering   Approved & own caterers.
Closed   Rarely.
Directions Directions on website.

£ £ £

Charlie & Emma Houston
Neen Sollars House, Neen Sollars,
Cleobury Mortimer DY14 0AH
Tel   +44 (0)1299 271556
Email events@zanzibarn.com
Web   www.zanzibarn.com

Walcot Hall

Dreamy gardens, a glorious lake, ornate fountains and one of the finest arboretums in the country. Despite the grandeur, 18th-century Walcot Hall exudes the comforts and charm of a much-loved family home. Stone lions watch with eyes half closed as you sashay into a polished hallway replete with Palladian columns and ancestral portraits. Marry here, or in the ballroom, all turquoise walls, candy coloured ceiling and sparkling chandeliers. Smaller groups can host ceremonies in the cosy drawing room with its stunning period ceiling, then dance the night away under twinkling lights in a secluded courtyard garden. Three-course wedding breakfasts, buffets and canapés are provided by professional caterers (no corkage fees). This vast house is a labour of love for the Parishes, and some bedrooms are yet to be revamped; the grand bridal suite in the main house is the pick of the bunch. In the grounds are several apartments including Muxton Chapel and the smart Dipping Shed (both sleep four), and a cute showman's caravan. You are looked after by the engaging Lucinda and her staff. Relaxed, and utterly unassuming.

Room hire	3 + marquee: Board (max 12). Cabaret (max 150). Theatre (max 100). Reception (max 200).
Catering	Approved & own caterers.
Sleeps	65: 25 B&B; 40 S/C.
Closed	Never.
Directions	From Shrewsbury A49 south to Craven Arms. Right onto B4368. Right to Lydbury North B4385 thro' village, left after Powis Arms pub.

Maria Higgs
Lydbury North,
Bishop's Castle SY7 8AZ

Tel	+44 (0)1588 680570
Email	enquiries@walcothall.com
Web	www.walcothall.com

Eaton Manor

Narrow lanes lace through South Shropshire's poppy-fringed fields, past a church and into this marvellously secluded family estate. For your larger celebration, choose Toad Hall, a grand, sleek, stone-built room clothed in solid oak and glass, with patio space to spill onto. A smaller party may choose from four other houses, the pick of the bunch being the 17th-century Manor House, with its gleaming oak table and four-poster beds. Or go the whole hog and hire the estate! Guests can pad back to the houses to sleep, then regroup the next day for a hangover breakfast and a spot of archery: there's an indoor, Olympic-size range and top-notch coaching on site. The pampering includes everything, from heated pool and croquet lawn to beauty treatments, murder mysteries and transport – in a limo if you like. But you're just as welcome to do your own thing, to self-cater, to explore the footpaths to Wenlock Edge. Secluded, friendly, country-style yet contemporary, this is great for all celebrations, hen parties, meetings, team-building weekends, a special break… Eaton ticks each and every category box.

Room hire	2: Board (max 18). Cabaret (max 50). Theatre (max 50). Reception (max 50).
Catering	In-house, approved & own caterers.
Sleeps	50: 2 S/C houses for 14; 1 S/C house for 12; 1 S/C house for 8; 1 S/C house for 2.
Closed	Never.
Directions	From Church Stretton B4371 to Wall-under-Heywood. Right past the Plough for 1.5 miles, left at T-junc, Eaton Manor on right.

Nichola Madeley
Eaton-Under-Heywood,
Church Stretton SY6 7DH

Tel	+44 (0)1694 724814
Email	nichola@eatonmanor.co.uk
Web	www.eatonmanor.co.uk

Iscoyd Park

Philip and Susie have returned to the old, very beautiful family home, lavishing it with much needed love and blowing away its 18th-century cobwebs. Their youth and enthusiasm shines through, while a sense of graceful old age remains. Rooms are elegant with antiques, gilt-framed art and fresh walls. The living room is a great spot to relax in – perhaps with a drink in front of the log fire – while the garden room is a focal point for weddings or civil ceremonies; high ceilings and arches pull in the light, and guests can wander through to the marquee on the lawn to join the happy couple. Professional chef Susie ensures that carefully chosen caterers produce delicious food, and, with Philip, makes sure all goes without a hitch on the day. Calming bedrooms with spoiling bathrooms mirror the simple refinement throughout. This is a hugely fun and welcoming place, a kind of home away from home, where the focus is on families gathered together; there's heaps of space to frolic in and even a creche for the tinies. When it's all over they plant a tree in your honour, for future generations to enjoy.

Room hire	3 + marquee: Board (max 30). Cabaret (max 120). Theatre (max 120). Reception (max 150).
Catering	Approved caterers.
Sleeps	6 B&B.
Closed	Rarely.
Directions	At Whitchurch take A525 Wrexham road to Wales. Then 1st right signed Iscoyd Park. After 1.4 miles house on right.

Philip & Susie Godsal
Whitchurch SY13 3AT
Tel   +44 (0)1948 780785
Email   info@iscoydpark.com
Web   www.iscoydpark.com

Combermere Abbey - The Glasshouse

Anticipation rises as you drive through the park of this ancient abbey on the Cheshire/Shropshire border. Cattle graze under spreading trees, a lake curves away into the distance. Soon you'll reach a secret garden enclosed by rosy brick walls, its five acres divided into inner gardens, all beautifully restored. Against the far wall is the pretty fan-shaped Glasshouse, approached via an intriguing fruit-tree maze (imagine it in blossom, marked by silken ribbons, with a bride threading her way through…). The Glasshouse is a magical setting for a wedding ceremony and not-too-big reception. Or, for larger events, hold the ceremony and champagne reception here, and the wedding breakfast in the elegant, contemporary Pavilion (in its own enchanting garden) next door. Family and friends can stay overnight, before and after the event, in the immaculate self-catering cottages in the turretted stable block; Stone Lodge, pleasingly Gothic, makes a great bridal suite. The Glasshouse is a delightful setting for all sorts of other celebrations and business gatherings, too; discuss what you want with warm, capable Serena.

Room hire	2: Board (max 24). Cabaret (max 150). Theatre (max 120). Reception (max 150).
Catering	Approved caterers.
Sleeps	31 S/C.
Closed	24, 25, 26 December. Pavilion not available January & February.
Directions	At junction of A530 and A525, follow signed entrance down 1 mile drive to Glasshouse. Rail station Crewe 11 miles. Directions on website.

Serena Cowell
Keepers Cottage, Combermere Abbey,
Whitchurch SY13 4AJ

Tel	+44 (0)1948 871662
Email	events@combermereabbey.co.uk
Web	www.combermereabbey.co.uk

Map 6

Porlock Vale House

Bring family and friends for a celebratory house party and soak up the Agatha Christie-esque atmosphere. Dramatic landscapes surround this imposing Edwardian hunting lodge, so scale the vertiginous heights of Porlock Hill and head to the remote western weir, where, between the sea and the wooded slopes of Exmoor, sits Porlock Vale House against a variegated burst of trees. All this to the gentle soundtrack of sea breaking on shingle, pheasants croaking and the piping of shoreline wading birds. Inside is warm and inviting – rich colours, dark polished woods, beamed ceilings, roaring fires, hunting portraits, stag heads, oak panelled walls, a 30-seater dining room (ask about a marquee if you need to extend your numbers). There are good local caterers, and a well-equipped kitchen if you prefer to go it alone; a snug leather lined bar and games room; and, upstairs, *Country Life* flounce in charming, comfortable bedrooms. Wander out onto wide lawns stretching towards the sea through 12 acres of grounds, and find all the traditional country pursuits – and more: extreme sports such as cliff leaping can be arranged.

Room hire	Whole house: Board (max 30). Reception (max 30).
Catering	Approved & self-catering.
Sleeps	30 S/C.
Closed	Never.
Directions	West past Minehead on A39, then right in Porlock, for Porlock Weir. Through West Porlock, signed right.

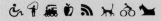

	Kim & Helen Youd
	Porlock Weir TA24 8NY
Tel	+44 (0)1643 862338
Email	info@porlockvale.co.uk
Web	www.porlockvale.co.uk

Bindon Country House

Bindon is a baroque fantasy, its curlicued façade, clad in wisteria and jasmine, overlooking seven acres of garden and woodland echoing with birdsong. This 17th-century house on the Somerset-Devon borders revels in the grandeur of its vaulted, tapestry-clad hallway – perfect for small wedding ceremonies with a wide staircase for the bride to sweep down. Living rooms, redolent of wood and open fires, are grand but not intimidating; the large dining room and orangery suit anything from presentations and business meetings to celebratory banquets. Bedrooms burst with colour and character, a four-poster here, a canopy bed there; bathrooms are equally opulent. Lynn has run Bindon for 12 years, and works with five full-time staff to organise events of all kinds. Chef Mike Davis uses local, seasonal ingredients to prepare meals great and small, but steps back if weekend house-party groups prefer to do their own thing. A terrace at the front of the house runs down to the lawn with plenty of room for a marquee; a heated pool, croquet lawn and all-weather tennis court are all to hand; other outdoor sports are nearby.

Room hire	4 + marquee: Board (max 24). Cabaret (max 50). Theatre (max 50). Reception (max 120).
Catering	In-house, approved & own caterers.
Sleeps	24 B&B, DB&B or S/C.
Closed	Rarely.
Directions	From Wellington, B3187 for 1.5 miles; left at sharp S-bend for Langford Budville; right for Wiveliscombe; 1st right; on right.

Lynn Jaffa
Langford Budville,
Wellington TA21 0RU

Tel	+44 (0)1823 400070
Email	stay@bindon.com
Web	www.bindon.com

Hestercombe Gardens

In rolling farmland, yet minutes from Taunton town centre, is a horticultural gem: three historic gardens spanning three centuries. While Hestercombe House is out of bounds, its 40 acres of gardens, lakes, waterfalls and follies form a beautiful backdrop to parties, weddings and meetings of all sizes. What's more, the gardens, open to the public all year round, are yours once the gates close at 5.30. Marry in the pretty Orangery, a classical hamstone building overlooking the formal Edwardian garden, and sip champagne on the Victorian terrace. The Landscape Garden's charming temple suits small ceremonies while the grander (but delightfully unintimidating) Bampfylde Hall, its rough plastered walls hung with ancestral portraits, can seat up to 150 guests (for meetings too). The lawn is big enough for a large marquee, the Courtyard is perfect for music, dancing and dining, and a bevy of chefs can produce seasonal Somerset-sourced meals, from a simple ploughman's buffet to a fabulous banquet. The ancient mill and barn, just-restored, provides further elegant-but-easy settings for events of all kinds.

Room hire	7 + marquee: Board (max 50). Cabaret (max 60). Theatre (max 140). Reception (max 150).
Catering	In-house catering.
Closed	Christmas Day.
Directions	Exit M5 junc. 25, follow signs for Taunton then follow Brown Daisy signs to Hestercombe Gardens, Cheddon 5 miles.

Sally Bennett
Cheddon Fitzpaine,
Taunton TA2 8LG

Tel	+44 (0)1823 413923
Email	sallybennett@hestercombe.com
Web	www.hestercombe.com

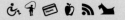

Maunsel House

Sweep down the yew-lined drive to your very own 13th-century manor house. Virginia creeper, clematis and roses riot; dogs, doves and peacocks greet you and Sir Ben and Kirsty throw open their doors. You can marry in a light-strewn gold and creamy Georgian ballroom, all ornate mirrors and dripping chandeliers, leading to immaculate lawns or marquee; or outdoors in a pretty gazebo. Inside, Kirsty has worked magic with Farrow & Ball paints and fresh flowers to brighten a treasure trove of heirlooms – ancestral portraits, butterfly collections and the Slade coat of arms. Dine under the stars in the secluded pergola or snuggle up in the bar with its open fire, then skip upstairs to pretty four-posters, a jacuzzi bath, chaise longues, ornate writing desks… and the King's Room bridal suite with high vaulted ceilings and an 8'x 6' bed draped in damasks and silks. Next morning, breakfast on fresh eggs at a magnificent, solid walnut table. Lounge in the library crammed with delights from Chinese vases to a stuffed bear; stroll around the woodland walk. Don't hold back: this place was made for parties.

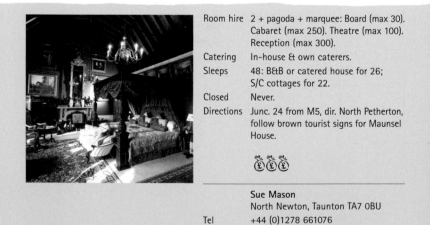

Room hire	2 + pagoda + marquee: Board (max 30). Cabaret (max 250). Theatre (max 100). Reception (max 300).
Catering	In-house & own caterers.
Sleeps	48: B&B or catered house for 26; S/C cottages for 22.
Closed	Never.
Directions	Junc. 24 from M5, dir. North Petherton, follow brown tourist signs for Maunsel House.

Sue Mason
North Newton, Taunton TA7 0BU
Tel   +44 (0)1278 661076
Email   info@maunselhouse.co.uk
Web   www.maunselhouse.co.uk

Huntstile Organic Farm

Marry in the foothills of the Quantocks in a pretty marquee on the lawn; feast on delicious and beautifully presented food, much of it home-grown. For a rustic wedding in organic style on a working farm, John – born and bred here – can whisk you off to church in a flower-decked tractor-drawn trailer replete with straw bales, and back for a hog roast and a Ho-Down. There's a stone circle too, perfect for a hand-fasting ceremony. But this is not only a summer place: the Jacobean panelled farmhouse with its cosy log-fired dining room is lovely for winter parties and weddings too. Or come for a meeting or team-building day (complete with falconry workshop). There's sleeping room for family and friends in the welcoming old farmhouse (winding stairs for the nimble only) and in the smart modern Apple Loft and Cider House; or put up your tent in the camping field, where solar panel showers are fed from the farm's own spring. Wake to a wonderful breakfast (organic rashers, eggs from Lizzie's chickens). Huntstile Farm is an organic dream and Lizzie and John buzz with energy and enthusiasm. *No civil licence.*

Room hire	2 + marquee: Board (max 24). Cabaret (max 140). Theatre (max 160). Reception (max 140).
Catering	In-house catering.
Sleeps	28: 22 B&B; 6 S/C.
Closed	End December-beginning January.
Directions	M5 Junc. 24 , left at r'bout dir North Petherton. Follow signs for Goathurst & Broomfield, 2nd right to Goathurst. Huntstile 1 mile on right.

Ethical Collection: Environment; Community; Food. See page 208 for details

Lizzie Myers
Goathurst, Bridgwater TA5 2DQ
Tel   +44 (0)1278 662358
Email   huntstile@live.co.uk
Web   www.huntstileorganicfarm.co.uk

Yarlington House

Up a hidden Somerset lane, a mellow Georgian manor, set in a stunning mix of formal and informal gardens, surrounded by parkland and wide open views – yours for the day, as far as the eye can see. Gracious and grand, yet with the warmth of a family home, there's something to astound at every turn: authentic copies of 18th-century wallpapers, elegant antiques, fine portraits and paintings. Celebrate your wedding in the imposing Dining Room, which seats 30, with its richly coloured and tapestried walls, or the charming Music Room: light, airy and built for entertaining with long windows looking out on to the gardens; both rooms work beautifully for meetings and conferences, too. Expand the party into the Hall (all the rooms combined hold up to 90). Or, for larger numbers, book a marquee for the garden. The fragrant rose garden is a delight, and you can glide down the laburnum walk to marry under the apple pergola. Friendly and flexible owners Carolyn and Charles de Salis are ready to help with arrangements, from organising a carriage to delicious locally sourced food, even a brunch party the morning after.

Room hire	House + marquee: Board (max 20). Cabaret (max 400). Theatre (max 60). Reception (max 400).
Catering	Approved caterers.
Sleeps	8 B&B.
Closed	Never.
Directions	From Wincanton A371 to Castle Cary. 2nd left after Holbrook House then 3rd right (both signed Yarlington). First stone gateposts on left.

Bernard de Salis
Yarlington, Wincanton BA9 8DY

Tel	+44 (0)1747 838910
Email	b.desalis@btinternet.com
Web	www.yarlingtonhouse.com

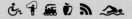

The Longhouse at Mill on the Brue

When Matt's parents arrived in 1982, this little valley on the edge of ancient Bruton was an ecological desert: an unloved, forlorn golf course scorched by years of chemical spraying. Little by little, the family has eased it back to life, planting thousands of trees and great stretches of hedgerow. They have been dogged in their refusal to use chemicals and have worked hard to entice bird and insect life back to what is now an outdoor education and activity centre (fear not, you have the whole 20 acres to yourself). At the heart of this lies their newest creation, the open-plan Longhouse. The interior is mute, calm, and flooded with light from the floor-to-ceiling windows that stretch along the whole of the southern edge. These fold open onto a full length balcony, beyond which are the valley and river that give this place its name. Packed with insulation and heated from under the floor via a ground-source heat pump, it's a warm, modern space in an enviable position. This is 'eco' without any hint of the hair shirt – perfect for stylish green weddings, conferences and team-building sessions. *Accommodation available.*

Room hire	2: Board (max 25). Cabaret (max 140). Theatre (max 80). Reception (max 140).
Catering	In-house catering. Locally sourced.
Closed	Christmas to New Year.
Directions	From Bath take A36 then A361 around Frome. Just past Frome turn left onto A359 for 8 miles. Nearest rail stations Bruton and Castle Cary.

Matt Rawlingson Plant
Trendle Farm, Tower Hill,
Bruton BA10 0BA

Tel	+44 (0)1749 812307
Email	info@longhouseweddings.co.uk
Web	www.longhouseweddings.co.uk

Ethical Collection: Environment;
Community; Food. See page 208 for details

Chalice Hill House

If the idea of a conventional top-hat-and-tails wedding fills you with dread, and there's a bit of the artist in you, a summer wedding party (or any other sort of celebration in this large Mughal tent) will be your bag. Find light colours, exotic lanterns, mirrored hangings, beautiful paintings and Turkish rugs. And the views from the Love Garden are stunning. You can see St John's spire poking out over the treetops, and Glastonbury buzzing below. Comfy U-shaped seating can be arranged, delicious food (if you want it brought in) is sourced locally, and you can put your own cooking tent up. In the Georgian house, Fay's contemporary artistic flair mingles naturally with the classical frame; grand mirrors, wooden floors, gentle colours and loads of books create an interesting feel. Bedrooms are enchanting; carved oak sleigh beds, embroidered Indian bedspreads and views of the dovecote, the wedding cake tree and Chalice Hill beyond. Camping is allowed in the garden; breakfasts are leisurely and served with panache. Exotic, comfortable elegance, a lovely hostess and a truly happy mood. *No civil licence.*

Room hire	Marquee: Cabaret (max 100). Theatre (max 100). Reception (max 100).
Catering	In-house catering. Locally sourced.
Sleeps	10 B&B.
Closed	Rarely.
Directions	From top of Glastonbury High Street, right; 2nd left into Dod Lane. Past Chalice Hill Close; right into driveway.

£ £ £

Fay Hutchcroft
Dod Lane, Glastonbury BA6 8BZ

Tel	+44 (0)1458 830828
Email	mail@chalicehill.co.uk
Web	www.chalicehill.co.uk

Stoberry House

A super coach house surrounded by 26 acres of parkland, but within walking distance of Wells; wherever you choose to get married (there's a choice of denominations in town, including the cathedral) you can stroll back for canapés on Stoberry's terrace… and a clever marquee that makes the most of the views; they're stunning. Smaller parties have a gorgeous 40-foot drawing room. Arrangements are flexible and Frances can help, so whether your heart's desire is a lavish bash or something quieter on a shoestring, just ask. Food can be sorted in or out of house, depending on numbers; waiting staff can be rustled up too. The gardens here are special all year round, and filled with art; a small marquee can be set up in the walled garden where photos should be perfect. Treat yourselves to a night or two in the Lady Hamilton room with its candlelit four-poster and Italian tiled bathroom – delicious for those in love – or whisk yourselves off to a hotel and come back to join family and friends for breakfast. This is lovely for house parties too – but best avoided during the Glastonbury Festival! *No civil licence.*

Room hire	1 + marquee: Board (max 12). Cabaret (max 200). Reception (max 200).
Catering	Approved & own caterers.
Sleeps	10 B&B.
Closed	Rarely.
Directions	A39 from Bristol, enter Wells, left into College Rd. Immediately left into Stoberry Park, follow track to Stoberry House at top of park.

Ethical Collection: Community.
See page 208 for details

	Frances Young Stoberry Park, Wells BA5 3LD
Tel	+44 (0)1749 672906
Email	stay@stoberry-park.co.uk
Web	www.stoberry-park.co.uk

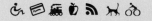

Roaches Hall

Take a deep breath — you've left city life well and truly behind. This is on the very edge of the Peak District: below gleams a wide expanse of water, above are dramatic crags. This is a big comfortable Victorian house with grand reception rooms, delightfully diverse bedrooms and informal gardens. (They've just planted 6,000 daffodils, so come in the spring.) The house is all yours but cheery, professional Sue will help to organise whatever you want, from business meetings and training events to small, perfect wedding receptions, house parties and celebrations of all sorts. Up to 40 can sit in the lovely dining room with its three round tables and balloon-backed chairs. Hire Sue's excellent caterer — who uses local produce and doesn't charge corkage — or be independent: a nearby supplier will be happy to fill the fridge with local food and regional specialities. Smaller guests will enjoy the dolls' house and dressing-up box, as well as hunting for the descendants of Sir Brocklehurst's escaped wallabies (ask Sue!). Everything from five-course 'pukka' dinners to getting mucky on the moors... *No civil licence.*

Room hire	2: Board (max 40). Cabaret (max 40). Reception (max 40).
Catering	In-house & self-catering.
Sleeps	S/C house for 30.
Closed	Never.
Directions	From Leek A53 dir. Buxton for approx 4 miles, left into Upper Hulme. First left, then right after approx. mile. Right over grid, Hall at end of lane.

Sue Moore
Upper Hulme, Leek ST13 5NL

Tel	+44 (0)1260 226609
Email	info@partyhouses.co.uk
Web	www.partyhouses.co.uk

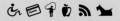

Tuddenham Mill

The historic mill's soaring chimney bursts up from Suffolk meadows and a swan-strewn pond; further buildings have been transformed into super-sleek function rooms, guest rooms and restaurant. Imaginative Italian design melds into a warm rusticity: mushroom, black and polished concrete against red brickwork, beams and the huge old mill wheel, fantastically up-lit at night. The first floor restaurant's giant beams and sisal flooring create a striking setting for a wedding breakfast or celebratory meal, the top table raised over the wheel; the Race Room suits an intimate dinner; casual lunches can be taken at the bar or water's edge. High up and light, the Terrace Room can hold a civil ceremony for 60 or a board meeting for 20. Dotted about the Mill and its gardens are 12 bedrooms that revel in their luxuriousness – goose down duvets, Bose sound systems, Jo Malone lotions… Swans, herons, kingfishers, deer are your neighbours, dogs are welcome, there's a boules court on site and Newmarket race course is close. It's sophisticated but informal, rural but city-chic, and yours for a fabulous occasion.

Room hire	4: Board (max 20). Cabaret (max 80). Theatre (max 40). Reception (max 120).
Catering	In-house catering.
Sleeps	24 B&B.
Closed	Rarely.
Directions	From A14 at junc. 38 exit onto A11 toward Thetford & Norwich. Right at Herringswell Rd, then on until High Street. Tuddenham Mill on the right.

Sarah Harrod
High Street, Tuddenham,
Newmarket IP28 6SQ

Tel	+44 (0)1638 713552
Email	info@tuddenhammill.co.uk
Web	www.tuddenhammill.co.uk

Entry 120   Map 4

Bruisyard Hall

This welcoming Suffolk country house is steeped in history; the west wing dates from 1364, the rest is a mere 450 years old. Mellow ancient oak floorboards and wonderful high-beamed ceilings have been enhanced by restoration work which uncovered Elizabethan fireplaces, lost windows, even a hidden room. Owners Robert and Teresa deal with bookings, and put you in touch with caterers and the like, but by and large you're left to your own devices to enjoy this splendid house and grounds. Wedding ceremonies and small parties take place in the aptly named Great Hall; larger receptions can be held in a marquee in the five-acre garden, against a backdrop of woodland, meadows and medieval fishpond. In the drawing room, sofas and armchairs cluster around a stone fireplace, fuelled by logs from the farm; relax in the snug or games room, eat in style or hold a meeting in the stately dining room. Up the 18th-century oak staircase, simple uncluttered bedrooms and bathrooms are kept spotlessly clean by housekeeper Val. If you're here for a celebratory house party, you can cook up a storm in the large well-equipped kitchen.

Room hire	3 + marquee: Board (max 22). Cabaret (max 150). Theatre (max 60). Reception (max 150).
Catering	Own caterers & self-catering.
Sleeps	20 B&B.
Closed	Never.
Directions	B118 off A12 at Saxmundham. Right at sharp left hand bend in Rendham. Right at T-junc. in Bruisyard, left at village sign. Hall 200 yds on right.

Robert & Teresa Rous
Bruisyard, Saxmundham IP17 2EJ

Tel	+44 (0)1728 638712
Email	dennington@farmline.com
Web	www.bruisyardhall.co.uk

The Old Rectory

A traditional country rectory from the outside with a contemporary edge within: modern artwork, a 21st-century orange chaise longue, fabulously dressed windows and the odd eclectic piece of antique or exotic furniture from Michael and Sally's time in the far east. The lovely dining room with stripped floor, open fire and a vast long table is just the ticket for a weekend house party of 20. Family gatherings, shooting parties and small weddings can have their celebratory feast in the huge stone-flagged conservatory where doors open onto two acres of orchard and lawns; there is a gate from the parish church next door and a superb lawn for a large marquee. Move onto the super terrace with big pots and long teak table for a starry supper party; delicious local, organic and seasonal dinners can be prepared for parties of over ten and there's a full licence. Bedrooms are pretty and smart; one overlooks the church, another has a claw-foot bath, and there is a romantic little cottage in the garden. Sutton Hoo and music venue Snape Maltings are close; shooting, sea fishing, golf and riding too. A happy house.

Room hire	2 + marquee: Board (max 20). Cabaret (max 40). Reception (max 130).
Catering	In-house catering. Locally sourced.
Sleeps	14 B&B.
Closed	Occasionally.
Directions	North from Ipswich on A12 for 15 miles, then right onto B1078. In village, over railway line; house on right just before church.

Michael & Sally Ball
Station Road, Campsea Ashe,
Woodbridge IP13 0PU

Tel	+44 (0)1728 746524
Email	mail@theoldrectorysuffolk.com
Web	www.theoldrectorysuffolk.com

The Barn

An away-from-it-all experience – rural peace, complete seclusion – amid the sleekest of 21st-century comforts. At this light-filled Tudor threshing barn (all dizzying height and ancient rafters), down a dead-end country lane yet only ten miles from Ipswich, nothing can disturb your fun or business focus: it's perfect for parties, meetings, exhibitions and receptions. Carefully renovated with huge windows, a floor-to-ceiling glazed entrance and subtle spotlights, the barn's cream walls, exposed timbering and heated limestone floor are awash with light. There's an oak-floored, book-lined 'minstrels' gallery' for musical entertainment, rehearsals or smaller meetings; a top-notch business presentation kit; a chic loft-style apartment for one lucky couple; and a purpose-designed space for caterers rustling up a banquet. Surrounded by lawns, meadows and woodland, summer guests can spill into the open-sided Gather Barn with its courtyard, while the knot garden, rose arch and ponds are perfect for party pictures. Owners Jane and Adrian are warmly efficient and passionate perfectionists. *No civil licence.*

Room hire	2: Board (max 30). Cabaret (max 50). Theatre (max 100). Reception (max 150).
Catering	Approved & own caterers.
Sleeps	2 B&B.
Closed	Christmas.
Directions	North of Woodbridge on A12, take road signed Bredfield. At T-junc. with B1078 (3 miles), left, then 1st right into Martins Lane. Farm House on right.

Adrian & Jane Stevensen
Valley Farm House, Clopton,
Woodbridge IP13 6QX

Tel	+44 (0)1473 737872
Email	info@thebarnsuffolk.co.uk
Web	www.thebarnsuffolk.co.uk

Kesgrave Hall

Sweep up the drive to this good-looking Georgian mansion sitting in 38 acres of woodland near Suffolk's magical coast. It served as home to US airmen during WWII, then became a prep school; recently refurbished, it shines in contemporary splendour and is ideal for meetings, awaydays, team building and private parties. Get stuck into great activities on the lawn: archery, laser clay pigeon shooting and 'it's a knockout' can all be laid on. The Mess, with French windows onto gardens, has all the latest gizmos and is superb for private parties; the Lodge, with two boardrooms for 16-18, is equally well geared up: surround sound, plasma screens, break-out areas and a kitchen for working lunches. There's a huge sitting room, and an airy, humming brasserie with a terrace. Excellent bedrooms have warm colours, crisp linen, super bathrooms. One is huge and comes with a zebra sofa and free-standing bath, some are in the eaves, others overlook the lawn. Dig into tasty, local food; this is more a restaurant with rooms and the emphasis is on good food served informally. But make no mistake – everything runs like clockwork.

Room hire	3: Board (max 24). Reception (max 40).
Catering	In-house catering.
Sleeps	46 B&B.
Closed	Never.
Directions	Skirt Ipswich to the south on A14, then head north on A12. Left at 4th roundabout; signed right after 0.25 miles.

Garth Wray
Hall Road, Kesgrave, Ipswich IP5 2PU
Tel   +44 (0)1473 333741
Email   reception@kesgravehall.com
Web   www.milsomhotels.com

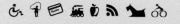

The Place at the Beach

A boutique hotel on the beach – friendly, stylish, chilled. Across the road, enormous dunes tumble down to Camber Sands for two miles of uninterrupted beach. Corporate awaydays are far from stuffy and usually come in extreme form: kite-surfing, go-karting, power-boating, a bareback horse gallop – but there are walks up to the river Rother, bird spotting and a spa nearby, too. Back at The Place, bright and airy meeting rooms come in light colours with screens and WiFi throughout. Or you can meet in the 'garden room' with its own private deck. Fancy an informal relaxed wedding with a driftwood theme? Want to have an unforgettable party on the beach? The super cool and charming Tudor can make it happen. Menus made for sharing and grazing offer local and retro style food: dover sole, mackerel and shellfish fresh from the market, a barbecue in summer – and bacon baps to keep the partygoers going till the early hours. For smaller parties there's a colourful yurt, and there's room for a marquee, too. Retire to comfy-smart bedrooms and spotless bathrooms after a hard day's partying or on the beach.

Room hire	4 + marquee + yurt: Board (max 85). Cabaret (max 200). Theatre (max 150). Reception (max 250).
Catering	In-house catering. Locally sourced.
Sleeps	37 B&B.
Closed	Never.
Directions	A259 east from Rye, then B2075 for Camber & Lydd. On left after 2 miles.

Tudor Hopkins
New Lydd Road, Camber,
Rye TN31 7RB

Tel	+44 (0)1797 225057
Email	enquiries@theplaceatthebeach.co.uk
Web	www.theplaceatthebeach.co.uk

Strand House

You could do a lot worse than hurl all your arrangements at bright, bubbly Mary; she's been doing house parties and small weddings for years and is expert at knowing when you need cossetting and when to give you space. Inside, party in the Inglenook room, low-ceilinged, and cosy, with fireplace and large glass doors leading out to the pretty garden where a marquee can happily sit; a comfortable lounge is filled with squashy chairs for relatives or friends with aching feet, and an honesty bar will be a lifeline to some. Concoct a toothsome menu of local and seasonal food with the chef patron; fish is straight off the boat. Bedrooms vary in size, but all are comfortable and one's a four-poster; small bathrooms are filled with good things. The road can be heard from the garden, but there are woodland trails and a path to old Winchelsea, and bird-filled marshlands to the sea wall; Mary can even organise a treasure hunt for your party. This was originally the workhouse (painted by Turner and Millais), and would have been on the seafront in the 14th-century: find twisting, uneven staircases and low doors.

Room hire	1 + marquee: Board (max 10). Cabaret (max 50). Theatre (max 25). Reception (max 50).
Catering	In-house catering.
Sleeps	23 B&B.
Closed	Mon–Thurs, 4 January–12 February.
Directions	A259 west from Rye for 2 miles. House on the left at foot of hill, opposite Bridge Inn pub.

Mary Sullivan & Hugh Davie
Tanyards Lane, Winchelsea TN36 4JT

Tel	+44 (0)1797 226276
Email	info@thestrandhouse.co.uk
Web	www.thestrandhouse.co.uk

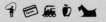

Wadhurst Castle

This is a real English castle, turreted and crenellated, with glorious flower-filled gardens and a suit of armour in the hall. High ceilings, wide corridors and gleaming parquet floors are grand but not intimidating thanks to the friendly feel of this family home. The ground floor and 140-acre estate are all yours for meetings, celebrations and weddings. The Drawing and Moncrieff Rooms, decorated in classic Regency style, are perfect for formal meals, presentations and receptions, while the magical Winter Garden, crammed with exotic plants, suits sumptuous candlelit dinners and intimate wedding ceremonies. For large gatherings, a marquee fits the lawn with room to spare; event manager Georgina can suggest caterers to conjure up your wildest dreams. Behind the castle lie vast lawns, endless South Down views, fairytale gardens, whimsical fountains, a rose garden ablaze with yellow and orange and a bloom-laden pergola. White magnolias frame the entrance to the walled garden – a bewitching setting for events of all kinds. Retire for the night to the Castle Cottage in the grounds.

Room hire	3 + marquee: Board (max 30). Cabaret (max 200). Theatre (max 60). Reception (max 200).
Catering	Approved caterers.
Sleeps	S/C cottage for 8.
Closed	Rarely.
Directions	Wadhurst Station 1 mile; bus stop outside gates. From Tunbridge Wells A267, in Frant left onto B2099 (Wadhurst). Gates opp. left turn to Lamberhurst.

£ £ £

Susanna Fitzgerald
Wadhurst TN5 6DA

Tel	+44 (0)1892 784262
Email	info@wadhurstcastle.co.uk
Web	www.wadhurstcastle.co.uk

Newick Park Hotel & Country Estate

A heavenly country house that thrills at every turn. The setting – 255 acres of parkland, river, lake and gardens – is spectacular. Inside, majestic interiors never fail to elate, be they colour-coded bookshelves in a panelled study, Doric columns in a glittering drawing room or roaring fires in the hall. You get all the aristocratic fixtures and fittings – grand piano, plaster mouldings, a bar that sits in an elegant alcove. Oils hang on walls, chandeliers dangle above. Marry outside in a flower-strewn loggia, celebrate with champagne and soak up the views from the terrace that run down to the lake. Peacocks roam freely and there are charming spots galore for perfect photos. The house is yours, so throw a party and twirl the night away. A great place to hole up for meetings and conferences too, and you'll find all the necessary gizmos and scrumptious working lunches; a two-acre walled garden provides much for the table. Top it off with some boisterous team-building – anything from treasure hunts to tank driving. Bedrooms are the stuff of dreams with views to the front of nothing but undulating countryside.

Room hire	3: Board (max 40). Theatre (max 100). Cabaret (max 74). Reception (max 150).
Catering	In-house. Own caterers for special requirements.
Sleeps	32 B&B.
Closed	New Year's Eve & New Year's Day.
Directions	From Newick village turn off the green & follow signs to Newick Park for 1 mile until T-junction. Turn left; after 300 yds, entrance on right.

Michael & Virginia Childs
Newick, Lewes BN8 4SB

Tel	+44 (0)1825 723633
Email	bookings@newickpark.co.uk
Web	www.newickpark.co.uk

Park House Hotel

A dreamy setting for a charming, country wedding. This warm Edwardian house sits in 12 green acres, with croquet on the lawn, a grass tennis court, shrubs and roses in well-kept beds, and a six-hole golf course that slips into the country... come to unwind in the boundless peace of an English garden. As for the house, it's as good as the garden: warm, peaceful and utterly spoiling. Wedding parties have the run of the place, including a delightful barn cleverly split in two – one half to host your civil ceremony, the other to eat and dance in. Lovely staff are on hand to transform the barn with fresh flowers, crisp linen, flickering candles and a delicious three-course meal; there's heaps of room for a live band or DJ too. A light-strewn conference room with WiFi and video conferencing looks onto rolling countryside yet you're only one hour from London. Super bedrooms come in unremitting country style, and the airy cottage in the grounds is the ultimate bridal party hideaway (Apple Mac for movies, music, internet, TV). Best of all, the brand new spa has an indoor pool, treatment rooms, steam room and sauna.

Room hire	3: Board (max 12). Cabaret (max 54). Theatre (max 54). Reception (max 54).
Catering	In-house catering.
Sleeps	47: 44 B&B; 3 S/C.
Closed	Rarely.
Directions	South from Midhurst on A286. At sharp left bend, right (straight ahead), signed Bepton. Hotel on left after 2 miles.

Rebecca & James Coonan
Bepton, Midhurst GU29 0JB

Tel	+44 (0)1730 819000
Email	reservations@parkhousehotel.com
Web	www.parkhousehotel.com

Talton Lodge

Two huge tipis, a yurt, a grand mansion house, a converted barn, all in 20 acres inhabited by hens, pigs and sheep – a memorable setting for a team-building event, a celebration or a green wedding! Imagine the possibilities: woodcraft or survival skills workshops, archery, canoeing on the river Stour, sausage-making courses... or just a meeting and an al fresco hog roast. Olivia worked as a chef under London's most famous culinary names before returning to her childhood home; she cures ham and bacon, makes pasta, bread, jams, grows fruit and veg and is passionate about sustainable living. The main tipi – rough, earthy, warm, with seating areas around a central fire – lifts its skirts to create a shelter with fine views. The yurt is cosier with its turquoise sheep's wool interior, while the barn suits more formal meetings with a kitchen and table for 18. In summer, bell tents are erected in the kitchen garden and guests can bring their own (breakfast goodies and firewood provided). And if sleeping under canvas doesn't appeal, the barn has dorm-style beds. Seriously green, totally unique, and great fun. *No civil licence.*

Room hire	2 + 2 tipis: Board (max 20). Cabaret (max 120). Theatre (max 100). Reception (max 120).
Catering	In-house catering.
Sleeps	22 B&B in barn, yurts, bell tent & tipi.
Closed	Rarely.
Directions	From Stratford-upon-Avon head to Newbold-on-Stour, then take the Crimscote Road for half a mile.

Olivia Hatch
Newbold-on-Stour,
Stratford-upon-Avon CV37 8UB

Tel	+44 (0)7962 273417
Email	olivia@taltonlodge.co.uk
Web	www.taltonlodge.co.uk

Ethical Collection: Environment; Food.
See page 208 for details

Lower Shaw Farm

You may not expect a little oasis of fruit and vegetable gardens, hens, ducks, sheep and rare breed pigs on the outskirts of Swindon, but that's what you find at Lower Shaw Farm. Simplicity is the key, with the largest space in converted outbuildings, and, for those who stay the night, some very basic hostel-style bedrooms. Andrea and Matt will greet you with delicious home-baked cake; meals are wholesome and vegetarian, using home-grown produce. The rustically sweet Centre suits meetings and parties while the Playbarn is just that, with old cushions and a rope swing. If it's raining and you had planned to be outdoors, just decamp to the concrete-floored milking shed, perfect for juggling and boisterous activities. In the red-brick farmhouse, the Hayloft makes a light, serene space for group sessions or yoga, while the cosy Cat's Room is suitable for more intimate meetings. Your warm, friendly and engaging hosts care deeply for the environment and the community, and their ethical stance permeates every corner of this place. Don't expect wireless widgets or luxurious pampering! *Eco-friendly courses & breaks.*

Room hire	4: Board (max 45). Cabaret (max 30). Reception (max 30).
Catering	In-house & own caterers.
Sleeps	35 DB&B.
Closed	Rarely.
Directions	4 miles from Swindon town centre. See website for directions.

Ethical Collection: Environment; Community; Food. See page 208 for details

Andrea Hirsch
Old Shaw Lane, Shaw, Swindon SN5 5PJ
Tel   +44 (0)1793 771080
Email   enquiries@lowershawfarm.co.uk
Web   www.lowershawfarm.co.uk

The Vine Tree

With a fine store of ales and over 40 wines by the glass, the old water mill is a watering hole in every sense. Service is young, friendly and accomplished and your event here can be as dapper or as laid-back as you like. There are 2.5 flat acres for a marquee that can hold up to 800 guests for a wedding reception, antique fair or ball, while the pretty terrace with lion fountain, urns of flowers and a profusion of roses is perfect for smaller weddings, blessings, 21st-birthday parties, Bar Mitzvah and wakes. Inside all is inviting: deep red walls, candlelight and beams, an open fire; tables in the minuscule upstairs room are super-cosy and popular for private meetings. Catering is in-house, seasonal and delicious: memorable local roast sirloin of beef, fresh fish and lobster from Devon and Cornwall, hog roasts, barbecues and local game. Country pursuits abound round here, so sporting lunches are catered for, too: polo, shooting, walking at Westonbirt. Charming Tiggi is the consummate event organiser and transport and local accommodation can be arranged. A perfectly welcoming, wood-warmed inn.

Room hire	4 + marquee: Board (max 12). Cabaret (max 500). Theatre (max 500). Reception (max 800).
Catering	In-house catering.
Closed	Never.
Directions	From M4 junc. 17 take the A429 for Cirencester. After 1.5 miles left for Norton. There, right for Foxley. Follow road; on left.

Charles Walker & Tiggi Wood
Foxley Road, Norton,
Malmesbury SN16 0JP

Tel	+44 (0)1666 837654
Email	tiggi@thevinetree.co.uk
Web	www.thevinetree.co.uk

Sheldon Manor

Sweep down a stately lime avenue to a magnificent Grade I-listed manor house, set in immaculate gardens and fronted by a deep and ancient porch. Roses cascade over honeyed stone walls, lanterns illuminate old yews, a lion's head spouts into a Roman pool. To one side lies an enchanting 15th-century chapel, light streaming through leaded windows, swallows darting in and out. A bird would see the house hugged by yet more greenery – roses everywhere, orchards, a vast lawn, bluebell woods... and beyond, rolling Wiltshire countryside, with Chippenham just close by. It's hard to imagine a more spectacular place to celebrate. Your only difficulty is choosing where: in the splendid grandeur of the Great Hall, piano tinkling and panelled walls gleaming in firelight; or the imposing dining room; or, for smaller occasions, the Porch, Library, Study or sweet Annexe. Party in the Wedding Pavilion or a marquee; dress up the stone loggia for a more informal affair. Caroline makes the house shine in all its bounteous glory, and can take care of everything from food to self-catering accommodation in the grounds. Simply stunning.

Room hire	3 + marquee: Board (max 12). Cabaret (max 60). Theatre (max 60). Reception (max 100).
Catering	Approved caterers.
Sleeps	22 S/C.
Closed	Rarely.
Directions	M4 junc.17; A350 to Chippenham; Bumpers Farm r'bout 4th exit A420; first left (Chippenham Lane) then first right again. Chippenham rail 3 miles.

Caroline Hawkins
Chippenham SN14 0RG

Tel	+44 (0)1249 653120
Email	sheldonevents@btconnect.com
Web	www.sheldonmanor.co.uk

Wellington Barn

Undulating green Wiltshire countryside surrounds the barn complex on this family-owned farm. The 18th-century Old Barn, all oak beams, vaulted ceilings, red bricks and wooden floor is a warm backdrop for drinks receptions, wedding ceremonies and dances. The Main Hall is a soaring space, seating 230 for a wedding breakfast or celebratory meal, its bar area complete with large squashy leather sofas. Décor is unobtrusive, making this a blank canvas to decorate exactly as you want. One end of the Main Hall is glazed, its doors and windows opening to a generous patio with benches, tables and chairs for sun-kissed summer parties; beyond are meadows and woods to explore. In a state-of-the-art kitchen, two full-time chefs cook up a storm, anything from hog roasts to formal meals, using the best local ingredients. Owner David, dedicated and efficient, is your event organiser, conjuring up everything from the latest presentation gizmos for business meetings to clay pigeon shooting. A passionate environmentalist, he's in cahoots with a local brewer to turn the farm's barley into beer for guests. Delicious!

Room hire	3: Board (max 40). Cabaret (max 230). Theatre (max 180). Reception (max 230).
Catering	In-house catering.
Closed	Rarely.
Directions	From Devizes A361 to Calne, past golf course, down hill, right at x-roads to Calstone. Follow signs to Barn.

Dave & Jo Maundrell
Manor Farm, Calstone Wellington,
Calne SN11 8PY

Tel	+44 (0)1249 823222
Email	events@wellingtonbarn.co.uk
Web	www.wellingtonbarn.co.uk

The Bath Arms at Longleat

A 17th-century coaching inn on the Longleat estate in a village lost in the country; geese swim in the river, cows laze in the fields, lush woodland wraps around you. At the front the 12 apostles – a dozen pollarded lime trees – shade a gravelled terrace. You can marry in the local church or in the tiny congregational chapel (1556) down the road... then float back to sip champagne and mingle on the two huge stone patios separated by beds of lavender (ask about a marquee if you want to increase your numbers). Or party inside. For a sumptuous wedding breakfast, feast on pork reared by the hotel and vegetables from the kitchen garden. Inside are the best of old and new: worn flagstones and boarded floors mix with a stainless steel bar. Bedrooms and bathrooms are a treat, with bags of personality. The smart and airy skittle alley doubles as a meeting room, all natural light and squishy leather poufs; try the cosy Bradley Room for that small but important meeting. Pick any team-building activity and Sara can make it happen... even duck-herding! Longleat is at the bottom of the hill and the walk down is majestic. *No civil licence.*

Room hire	3: Board (max 12). Cabaret (max 50). Theatre (max 40). Reception (max 70).
Catering	In-house catering.
Sleeps	34: 30 B&B; S/C lodge for 4.
Closed	Never.
Directions	A303, then A350 north to Longbridge Deverill. Left for Maiden Bradley; right for Horningsham. Through village, on right.

Sara Elston
Horningsham, Warminster BA12 7LY

Tel	+44 (0)1985 844308
Email	enquiries@batharms.co.uk
Web	www.batharms.co.uk

 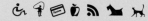

Bradley House

Celebrate in splendour in this luxurious Tudor house, seat of the Dukes of Somerset since the 1680s. In a charming Wiltshire village amid verdant countryside, this is a majestic setting for house parties, business do's, weddings... and family holidays; 24 can sleep soundly in sumptuous ease. Marry in the charming village church next door, or in the house that oozes history; imagine portraits, ancient tapestries, wood panelling and impeccable antiques at every turn. The dining room's mahogany table works beautifully for meetings and meals; blazing fires in the library and drawing room encourage languid relaxation; the music room's patio is perfect for drinks. You have exclusive use of the estate, from manicured parkland to wild forest, as well as the outdoor pool, the croquet lawn and the shepherd's hut for clay pigeon shooting. The stable block and coach house hide a bar, dance floor and chill-out area (hired independently of the house for one-day events and meetings); a marquee is attached. Friendly, efficient Kim and David will help plan events of any style, budget and size, and enlist the best local caterers.

Room hire	3 + marquee: Board (max 20). Cabaret (max 180). Theatre (max 210). Reception (max 210).
Catering	Approved & self-catering.
Sleeps	24: S/C or catered house.
Closed	Never.
Directions	Situated off B3092 in Maiden Bradley between Mere & Frome. Turn into Kingston Lane next to church. Bradley House is 300 yards on right.

David & Kim Mattia
Maiden Bradley, Warminster BA12 7HL

Tel	+44 (0)1985 844052
Email	info@bradleyhouse.org
Web	www.bradleyhouse.org

Sarum College

This is very much a working education college but the setting in the Cathedral Close is stunning. When your work is done and dusted you can listen to the choir sing at Evensong, stroll around the cathedral cloisters or wander to a good theatre or restaurant nearby. There are a number of conference and event rooms to choose from for business meetings, working lunches, special evening meals, birthday parties and small wedding receptions; Linda can arrange projectors, laptops, courses, high tea. The Cavell Room is an elegant space for a small celebratory party, while Butterfield Chapel, attached to the college, is a fine venue for a concert. There's a sitting room for guests and the seven bedrooms are plain and comfortable and all have views of the cathedral; bathrooms are functional and neat as a pin. Good, freshly prepared food is served in the Refectory, which seats up to 100 and can cater for special diets. In quiet moments browse the college's specialist bookshop or library; there is a common room and bar too. Peaceful, sedate, secluded and in the historic heart of the city. *No civil licence.*

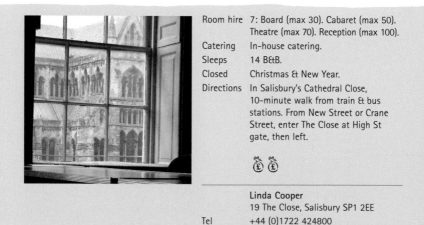

Room hire	7: Board (max 30). Cabaret (max 50). Theatre (max 70). Reception (max 100).
Catering	In-house catering.
Sleeps	14 B&B.
Closed	Christmas & New Year.
Directions	In Salisbury's Cathedral Close, 10-minute walk from train & bus stations. From New Street or Crane Street, enter The Close at High St gate, then left.

Linda Cooper
19 The Close, Salisbury SP1 2EE

Tel	+44 (0)1722 424800
Email	hospitality@sarum.ac.uk
Web	www.sarum.ac.uk

The Cottage in the Wood & Outlook Restaurant

A hugely welcoming hotel with an utterly magical view. The décor is not cutting-edge contemporary, but nor would you want it to be: this is a hotel where old-fashioned values win out. Service is charming, the sort you only get with a passionate family at the helm and a battalion of long-standing staff to back them up. Small, informal wedding receptions, special birthdays and anniversaries work wonderfully well, and fabulous food is served in a restaurant that drinks in the view – a winning formula for those who seek solid comfort rather than fly-by-night fashion. Two small but perfectly formed board rooms concentrate the mind: natural light, WiFi, screens, and a hearty working lunch taken on the terrace where views stretch for 30 miles to distant Cotswold hills. There are walks through light-dappled trees and team-building options galore: hawk flying, giant Scaletrix, quad biking nearby. Bedrooms are split between the main house (simple, traditional), the cottage (warm and snug) and the Pinnacles (hugely pleasing, good and spacious, the odd balcony). A pretty garden adds colour. *No civil licence.*

Room hire	3: Board (max 14). Cabaret (max 60). Theatre (max 20). Reception (max 60).
Catering	In-house catering.
Sleeps	60 DB&B.
Closed	Never.
Directions	M5 junc. 7; A449 through Gt Malvern. In Malvern Wells, 3rd right after Railway pub. Signed.

John & Sue Pattin
Holywell Road, Malvern WR14 4LG

Tel	+44 (0)1684 588860
Email	reception@cottageinthewood.co.uk
Web	www.cottageinthewood.co.uk

The Angel Inn

The Angel has it all – a perfect, family-run English inn. It stands in the middle of a tiny hamlet surrounded by lush fields with Rylstone Fell rising behind. Have your birthday celebration, anniversary party or small intimate wedding reception in the half-panelled bar, pop a bottle of champagne on the flower-festooned terrace and have a fabulous, French-inspired formal buffet or spit-roast feast in a choice of dining rooms. All the ancient trimmings are here – mullioned windows, beamed ceilings, exposed stone walls, working Yorkshire range – yet the feel is bright and breezy. Marry in the stone walled wine cave with its French vibe; all the wines are sourced from small French vineyards and wine tasting events flow. Above, you find exquisite bedrooms with a French armoire, a brass bed, murals or a claw-foot bath; honeymooners will be in the lap of luxury in the Rylstone suite. Expect the best fabrics, pretty colours, flat-screen TVs. Parties of 120 can spill over into the nearby village hall and everything from flowers and canapés to jazz bands, summer barbecues and outdoor pursuits can be arranged.

Room hire	4: Board (max 16). Cabaret (max 61). Theatre (max 50). Reception (max 100).
Catering	In-house catering.
Sleeps	10 B&B.
Closed	Christmas Day; 1 week in January.
Directions	North from Skipton on B6265. Left at Rylstone for Hetton. In village.

Juliet Watkins
Hetton, Skipton BD23 6LT
Tel   +44 (0)1756 730263
Email   info@angelhetton.co.uk
Web   www.angelhetton.co.uk

Knowles Lodge

Chris's father built this timber-framed house in 1938 in 18 acres of glorious hillside in the Yorkshire Dales. It's a comfortable, comforting and informal place to have a relaxed wedding. The dining and drawing rooms, joined by glass doors, can hold up to 100 guests, and in summer, you can marry on the covered, flower-decked terrace with stunning views and the scent of lavender wafting. Choose between a traditional marquee or an Indian style tipi on the back lawn; there's a curved staircase for swish photos. Honey walls and polished floors give the sitting room a light airy feel, deep sofas make it cosy, a fine collection of modern art adds interest and there are gorgeous views from large windows. Bedrooms are attractive with sprightly fabrics and fresh flowers. You're superbly well looked after: friendly Pam and Chris can advise on food, flowers, cakes, music, barrels of beer and more. They are happy to cook for up to 12, or local caterers will do buffets, a sit-down affair or a hog roast. Great walking, trout fishing, solitude – and camping in the meadow for hardy guests. *Minimum stay two nights for weddings.*

Room hire	2 + marquee, tipi: Cabaret (max 120). Theatre (max 12). Reception (max 120).
Catering	In-house & approved caterers.
Sleeps	6 B&B.
Closed	Never.
Directions	A59 to Bolton Abbey. At r'bout, B6160 Burnsall. 3 miles after Devonshire Arms, right immed. after B. Tower for Appletreewick. Down hill, over bridge, up hill, 0.75 miles. Cross bridge; on left.

	Pam & Chris Knowles-Fitton
	Appletreewick, Skipton BD23 6DQ
Tel	+44 (0)1756 720228
Email	pam@knowleslodge.com
Web	www.knowleslodge.com

The Devonshire Arms

An elegant, fabulous hotel — just follow your nose and find everything you could possibly hope for. Fires roar, staff swoop on luggage, beams hang overhead, there's a piano in the cocktail bar and a Michelin star in the dining room. This wonderful venue hosts impeccable, stylish weddings (and celebrations too). Marry in the beautiful, columned Cavendish room, the air perfumed by flowers, then glide over to the striking, portrait-filled Clifford room for a divine nine-course affair, or something simpler from the whitewashed brasserie if you prefer. You'll find a level of service that surpasses most others: a discreet concierge can magic up a chauffeur, butler, guided walks, private fishing on the river Wharfe, even hover-crafting. Across the road is a super swish spa (pool, sauna, steam, jacuzzi) and a walled kitchen garden with a bench by the stream, a sun-drenched spot for romantic photos. Modern country-house bedrooms are predictably sublime; try a high four-poster with stunning views of beautiful gardens and endless woodland and parkland beyond. One of the loveliest places to stay in the country.

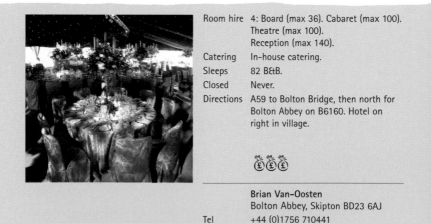

Room hire	4: Board (max 36). Cabaret (max 100). Theatre (max 100). Reception (max 140).
Catering	In-house catering.
Sleeps	82 B&B.
Closed	Never.
Directions	A59 to Bolton Bridge, then north for Bolton Abbey on B6160. Hotel on right in village.

Brian Van-Oosten
Bolton Abbey, Skipton BD23 6AJ

Tel	+44 (0)1756 710441
Email	brian.van-oosten@devonshirehotels.co.uk
Web	www.thedevonshirearms.co.uk

The General Tarleton

Envelop yourself in the warm comforts of this solidly handsome whitewashed 18th-century coaching inn, flanked by open fields and flagstoned gardens. Its bijou exterior deceives: the spacious and minimally chic foyer opens up to reveal, tardis–like, a sophisticated and well-ordered pub. Downstairs is a darkly hued snug and inviting bar with a huge open fire, and two dining rooms. One is cool and contemporary in a glass-roofed courtyard with stone tiled floors, the other, in the older part of the building, is more formal, with cream-painted wooden beams, upholstered chairs and a charming terrace garden. Upstairs, hold an intimate wedding breakfast for 40 or a celebratory party in the raftered, candelabra-lit function room, where tall-backed chairs hint at medieval style. Smart and comfortable bedrooms are spic 'n' span and you're in excellent hands on the food front; the team is headed by owner and fêted chef, John Topham, and his wife, Claire, ably supported by smiley Katie. She's run the place for years and will happily coordinate any event, be it a wedding, family gathering or business meeting.

Room hire	2 + whole pub: Board (max 22). Cabaret (max 40). Theatre (max 50). Reception (max 160).
Catering	In-house catering.
Sleeps	28 B&B.
Closed	Rarely.
Directions	From A1 junction 48; A6055 for Knaresborough; on right in Ferensby.

John Topham
Boroughbridge Road, Ferrensby,
Knaresborough HG5 0PZ

Tel	+44 (0)1423 340284
Email	gti@generaltarleton.co.uk
Web	www.generaltarleton.co.uk

The Grange Hotel

York is on your doorstep and its imperious Minster stands less than half a mile from the front door of this extremely comfortable Regency townhouse. A clipped country-house elegance runs throughout: a colonnaded portico outside, and inside, marble pillars in a flagged entrance hall, a series of formal reception rooms, and flowers everywhere. The panelled Morning Room suits board meetings; the Library joins up with the gracious first-floor Drawing Room, with a little balcony, for larger meetings. Or combine the light-flooded Green Room with the super-smart Ivy Brasserie to transform a theatre-style meeting venue into a stylish dining and mingling space for weddings and celebrations. Smaller weddings and meetings fit perfectly into the Alcove, just off the Brasserie. After the formalities are over, late partying can continue in the vaulted Cellar Bar downstairs. Put together your own menu from an extensive directory, with ingredients sourced locally wherever possible. The helpful events team are on hand to advise. Bedrooms come in different shapes and sizes, and the more expensive are seriously plush.

Room hire	5: Board (max 24). Cabaret (max 75). Theatre (max 50). Reception (max 120).
Catering	In-house catering.
Sleeps	71 B&B.
Closed	Never.
Directions	From A1237 outer ring road take A19 towards York City Centre. On right after two miles, 400 yards from city centre.

Suzanne Newman
1 Clifton, York YO30 6AA

Tel	+44 (0)1904 644744
Email	info@grangehotel.co.uk
Web	www.grangehotel.co.uk

Castle Howard

This stunning baroque extravaganza is the archetypal British stately home, the ultimate backdrop to a grand wedding or gala. When the public leave for the day, the immense house and its thousand majestic acres of Yorkshire parkland – temples, lakes, statues, fountains, walled garden crammed with roses and delphiniums, ancient woodland – are all yours. Relive your Brideshead fantasies! Marry in the Temple of the Four Winds, then celebrate in the magnificent Long Gallery or smaller Grecian Room, spilling out into the gardens on sunnier days; guests can even ply the lake in a renovated electric launch. Gather for champagne in the Great Hall and admire the antiques, statues, paintings and mementos collected by the Howard family on grand tours of Europe. A large dedicated kitchen produces hearty traditional cuisine for any number, with delicious local specialities. Events manager Lisa, warm and knowledgeable, can organise every aspect of your day, from cakes to vintage cars. You can even have a private guided tour of this splendid chunk of English history.

Room hire	5: Board (max 30). Cabaret (max 250). Theatre (max 200). Reception (max 250).
Catering	In-house catering.
Closed	Rarely.
Directions	From York, A64 signed Melton & Scarborough. Left onto Mains Lane, continue on The Stray. Castle Howard on right. Look for brown tourist signs.

Lisa Parker-Gomm
York YO60 7DA

Tel	+44 (0)1653 648623
Email	house@castlehoward.co.uk
Web	www.castlehoward.co.uk

The Durham Ox

At the picturesque top of the Grand Old Duke of York's hill is an L-shaped bar of flagstones and rose walls, worn leather armchairs and settles, carved panelling and big fires. With two more bars, a dapper wine-themed restaurant and an elegant boardroom with facilities, all is set for your cocktail party, wedding, working lunch or presentation. In-house catering offers good, seasonal three-course or buffet menus and barbecues. The Ox can come to you too: everything from full dinner to DJ can be delivered for your party; event planning, butler service, decorating and clearing can be orchestrated too. The church is a short stroll, there's a garden with a flower-filled marquee for summer weddings and birthday frivolity, and you can order a dazzling array of extra touches: bagpipes, fireworks, jazz bands and more. No need to drive home: four delightfully quirky bedrooms in the old farmworkers' cottages have been renovated in contemporary country-house style. The far-reaching views across the valley are stunning, flowers burst from stone troughs and the nearby castle provide great photo opportunities. *No civil licence.*

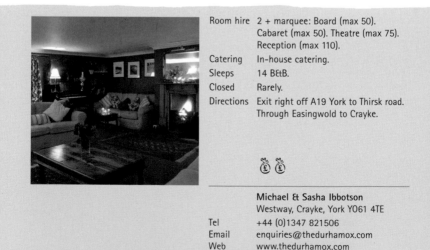

Room hire	2 + marquee: Board (max 50). Cabaret (max 50). Theatre (max 75). Reception (max 110).
Catering	In-house catering.
Sleeps	14 B&B.
Closed	Rarely.
Directions	Exit right off A19 York to Thirsk road. Through Easingwold to Crayke.

Michael & Sasha Ibbotson
Westway, Crayke, York YO61 4TE

Tel	+44 (0)1347 821506
Email	enquiries@thedurhamox.com
Web	www.thedurhamox.com

Feversham Arms & Verbena Spa

Perched prettily on the edge of the Moors, Helmsley is a classic Yorkshire market town with a handsome central square. This good-looking 1855 building stands behind the lovely old church and within walking distance of shops and tea rooms. Whether you want to take over the whole place for a wedding, meet with fellow workers for a meeting big or small, spend an active day bonding outdoors, or simply gather for a family reunion, you'll be cheerfully looked after by the competent staff. Plenty of space means you can choose from two private dining rooms, an enormous two-storey mezzanine reception area, a large boardroom and a searingly modern spa with an outdoor heated pool and a designer courtyard garden – super for pretty pictures and private parties. There's good modern art on the walls, an eclectic mix of furniture, and a restaurant deeply rooted in the local area. Sleeping here is a treat: super beds, beautiful fabrics, indulgent bathrooms. Yorkshire may have a slew of grand hotels but you'd be hard-pressed to find a more stylish one than this, a top favourite with our readers.

Room hire	4: Board (max 24). Cabaret (max 24). Theatre (max 35). Reception (max 110).
Catering	In-house catering.
Sleeps	66 B&B.
Closed	Never.
Directions	East from Thirsk on A170. In Helmsley, left at top of square & car park; hotel on right by church.

Simon & Jill Rhatigan
Helmsley, York YO62 5AG

Tel	+44 (0)1439 770766
Email	info@fevershamarmshotel.com
Web	www.fevershamarmshotel.com

Wales

Plas Glansevin

A splendid place for a big extended-family celebration, house party, wedding, retreat or mid-week corporate break: up to 62 can sleep comfortably in two houses. A marquee and tents for up to 150 can be set up, organic and local catering can be arranged, facilities for business events laid on; music, evening entertainment, even a magician will all be impeccably sorted. The Coach House bedrooms and bathrooms are simple and spacious, and the open-plan kitchen/sitting area is an attractive, convivial and well-equipped space with a high stone chimney for open fires and a mezzanine sitting area. The Mansion House is architecturally grander with an impressive, oak-floored, sunshine-yellow entrance hall that's perfect for dancing; simply furnished bedrooms overlook the lawn and wooded grounds. Expect shutters, period fireplaces, a good smattering of modern art and African and Indonesian furniture. The vast, rustic dining room for candlelit feasts has benches, or seating for conferences. There are games rooms, wood-burning saunas and plunge pools, outdoor activities for team-building, and the Brecon Beacons to discover.

Room hire	8 + marquee: Board (max 62). Cabaret (max 150). Theatre (max 36). Reception (max 150).
Catering	Approved & self-catering.
Sleeps	62: 1 S/C house for 39; 1 S/C house for 23.
Closed	Never.
Directions	Off A40 to Llangadog into village. Left opp. store. 50 yds right to Myddfai then 1.5 miles. Glansevin on left.

Harvey Peters
Llangadog SA19 9HY
Tel +44 (0)1550 777121
Email harveypeters@btinternet.com
Web www.glansevin.com

The Aeron Centre

When business sessions last more than a day you need great spaces to meet and sleep, and plentiful good food – which is exactly what Jack provides on his organic cattle and sheep farm set high above Ceredigion's rolling countryside. The old milking parlour has been transformed into an intimate three-room events space: the bright, modern Aeron Room, the smaller Beech Room (with projector), and the dining room where Jack serves home-cooked, locally sourced food. Although not far from Lampeter and public transport, the farm's self-catering accommodation is a definite bonus for those who need to stay: choose between the delightfully creaky thatched cottage with low ceilings, Welsh antiques and 1650s wall paintings, and one of the cottages; the old granary, carthouse and farmhouse have been smartly renovated. When work's done for the day, follow a trail through the farm or sit outside with a book and the breeze; if you want a snack or three-course meal Jack will produce that too! Combined with breathtaking views and the appeal of a working farm, your meetings will be both productive and happy.

Room hire	2: Board (max 20). Cabaret (max 24). Theatre (max 22). Reception (max 35).
Catering	In-house & self-catering.
Sleeps	27 B&B or S/C.
Closed	Rarely.
Directions	From Lampeter, take A475 then B4337 to Cribyn, cont. on B4337, after two miles turn left down a narrow lane to The Aeron Centre.

Jack Cockburn
Treberfedd Farm, Dihewyd,
Lampeter SA48 7NW
Tel +44 (0)1570 470672
Email info@treberfedd.co.uk
Web www.treberfedd.co.uk

Room to Think

Cocooned amidst beautiful countryside in West Wales, it's no wonder the Blacklers are so enthusiastic about their bright new eco-friendly meeting rooms and guest quarters. Meadows merge into glorious gardens, where you will discover half-hidden sculptures, heritage fruit trees, wild flowers, buzzing wildlife and a secluded clearing in the trees. Meetings, training workshops and celebrations mostly take place in a cleverly converted barn, small and sweet on the outside and opening to a spacious, modern interior lit by sun pipes; a bookcase covers one wall and gives way to a cosy sitting area. At mealtimes Liz produces delicious plates of home-cooked food, all locally sourced or from the organic garden. For small meetings or drinks the funky L-shaped pond-side retreat is just the ticket; there's also a petite summerhouse which can spin to face the sun. After a day in such peaceful and creative surroundings you may wish to stay... handily there are two options, a beautifully renovated stone cottage or a newly built barn. Friendly, competent Liz makes sure that everything runs to plan.

Room hire	2: Board (max 24). Cabaret (max 30). Theatre (max 50). Reception (max 50).
Catering	In-house catering. Fully organic.
Sleeps	11 B&B or S/C.
Closed	Never.
Directions	A484 to A486 from Camarthen to Ffostrasol; turn onto B4571 at Ffostrasol Tavarn. Up hill 0.5 miles, right-hand turn as hill levels off, signposted.

Liz Blackler
Castell, Ffostrasol, Llandysul SA44 5JS
Tel   +44 (0)1239 851851
Email   info@roomtothink.co.uk
Web   www.roomtothink.co.uk

fforest

Camping, but not as you know it. This is one of the most enchanting places for a party, an intimate wedding, even an informal business meeting, large or small. Those averse to gas stoves or mud underfoot, be happy: breakfast is a relaxed communal affair, there's a cedar barrel sauna and a solar-powered shower block. Tents – nomad, kata, or dome – are built on raised platforms to keep dry. The four adjoining 'croglofts' have underfloor heating, wood-burners and super porch kitchens that let the world in but keep out the rain. All has been designed in tune with nature and leaves the barest mark on the environment; rainwater is recycled, wood is reclaimed, loos are composted and clean. Team builders will love the activities, on and off site: bushcraft, surfing, canoeing, abseiling... more sybaritic souls can retreat to the lodge lounge for a coffee, explore the woodland or find a spot from which to soak in the views. Food is local and seasonal, perhaps a hog roast for hungry wedding guests; brides can calm pre-wedding nerves in their luxurious crog cottage before dancing the night away under the stars. Quite unique.

Room hire	2: Cabaret (max 100). Theatre (max 90). Reception (max 100).
Catering	In-house catering. Self-catering in tents.
Sleeps	108 S/C camping.
Closed	January & school holidays.
Directions	From Carmarthen A40 West to Penblewin r'bout. Third exit onto the A478. At Pen-y-Bryn turn right and follow brown signs for Canoe Trips.

James Lynch & Sian Tucker
Fforest Farm, Cilgerran SA43 2TB

Tel	+44 (0)1239 615209
Email	info@coldatnight.co.uk
Web	www.coldatnight.co.uk

Picton Castle

Grand wrought-iron gates complete with prancing lions welcome you to this impressive 13th-century edifice in the Pembrokeshire Coast National Park. Part fortified manor house, part medieval castle, dramatic towers enclose a charming Georgian interior. Marry in the pink Palladian splendour of the Great Hall, its entrance flanked by pillars and topped by a gallery; banqueting chairs replace the antique drawing room furniture for large weddings. The idiosyncratic Circular Library, hidden in a tower, suits smaller ceremonies, with a fully equipped bride's room across the hall. Hold meetings in the magnificent Regency dining room, and exhibitions or business events in the whitewashed Gallery, an ex-outbuilding. Forty acres of beautiful gardens, home to some of the most ancient trees in West Wales, are yours; spring and summer see the woodland carpeted with flowers. The 19th-century walled garden with fountain and rose-laden arches makes a stunning backdrop for photos, and there's space on the lawn for a marquee. Wedding planner Rossita and chef Maria organise every aspect of your day – but go it alone if you prefer.

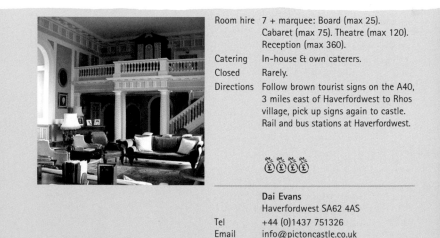

Room hire	7 + marquee: Board (max 25). Cabaret (max 75). Theatre (max 120). Reception (max 360).
Catering	In-house & own caterers.
Closed	Rarely.
Directions	Follow brown tourist signs on the A40, 3 miles east of Haverfordwest to Rhos village, pick up signs again to castle. Rail and bus stations at Haverfordwest.

Dai Evans
Haverfordwest SA62 4AS

Tel	+44 (0)1437 751326
Email	info@pictoncastle.co.uk
Web	www.pictoncastle.co.uk

Slebech Park

An imperious position on the upper reaches of Daugleddau Estuary, this crenellated building, dating from 1760, forms part of a 600-acre estate and stands 30 paces from the water; gaze on river, wood and migrating birds stopping for a bathe. You have landed in the lap of luxury here, the perfect setting for a grand house party or dinner dance, business gathering or wedding. Charmingly suave Geoffrey and his excellent event team provide a marquee for summer and winter weddings, a choice of rooms for champagne and canapés, a roaring log fire. Rooms and suites are sublime: grand yet contemporary and chic. You get vast sofas, padded window seats, beautiful colours, huge beds wrapped in white linen, fancy bathrooms. One on the ground floor has fine arched windows opening onto a terrace. There's a super kitchen and a rather good restaurant too, for Welsh beef, fish from local waters, game from the estate. All manner of team-building and sporting activities can be arranged, while corporate events have state-of-the-art facilities. Then there are the breathtaking gardens and the sunny courtyard for summer partying... perfect.

Room hire	4 + marquee: Board (max 60). Cabaret (max 180). Theatre (max 300). Reception (max 400).
Catering	In-house catering.
Sleeps	30 B&B or DB&B.
Closed	Never.
Directions	M4, then A48 & A40 west. Through Slebech (5 miles east of Haverfordwest) and 1st left. Lodge on left after a mile.

Geoffrey & Georgina Phillips
Slebech, Haverfordwest SA62 4AX

Tel	+44 (0)1437 752000
Email	enquiries@slebech.co.uk
Web	www.slebech.co.uk

Weddings • Parties • Meetings • Conferences

Felin Newydd House

A country pad par excellence – nothing does justice to this metamorphosis of substantial country house into decadent 21st-century retreat. Sweeping through the grand hallway, prepare to be dazzled by light streaming through the angular cupola. It's an exceptional house for weddings and house parties – come with as many friends as you can muster! Lord and lady it over the 50-acre estate – shooting parties can be arranged and house staff brought in to attend to every whim. Bridal couples may plump for the four-poster but each bedroom has its charm – old leather suitcases, a glossy chaise longue – while a feminine eye has added strong pinks, tactile fabrics, glamorous bathrooms and fresh flowers. Take supper in the Aga-toasty kitchen, or dine at a mahogany table in the silk-draped drawing room – worth dressing up for. There are the morning room (just right for brainstorming sessions) and the billiard room to retreat to, and the garden to stroll. On the site of a 17th-century mill, the peachy-pink house is near the Brecon Beacons and Black Mountains. Pull on the boots and gorge-walk, fish and canoe.

Room hire	2 + marquee: Board (max 20). Cabaret (max 150). Theatre (max 60). Reception (max 150).
Catering	Approved & own caterers.
Sleeps	18 B&B.
Closed	Rarely.
Directions	Off A470 between Brecon and Builth Wells.

Huw Evans Bevan & Elizabeth Saevareide
Llandefalle, Brecon LD3 0NE

Tel	+44 (0)1874 754216
Email	info@countrypad.co.uk
Web	www.countrypad.co.uk

Penpont

Penpont is lovely: Grade I-listed with slated roofs, walls a comforting patchwork of old stone, beautiful grounds. And Vina and Gavin are the nicest people. Surrounded by 2,000 acres of farm and woodland, a maze, lawns and gardens, with the river Usk running through, this is a peaceful, beautiful place for workshops, conferences, yoga retreats, performances and weddings. The Stable Room — brick floor, chunky oak tables, wood-burner and modern kitchen — seats up to 80; the rustic Museum Room is smaller; art workshops can be held in the warm yellow l-shaped room; and the beamed, oak-floored Hayloft and Grainstore are perfect for theatre, dances and meetings. There are lovely spots everywhere for reception drinks and ceremonies: an ornate walled garden, an old rose garden, a six-pointed awning, and the big house itself; plenty of parking and disabled access too. The self-catered courtyard wing is cosy, well-decorated and generous, and can be hired exclusively. Vina recommends local caterers; organic produce from the estate can to used too. Walks galore, tennis, fly fishing, swimming: Welsh heaven. *No civil licence.*

Room hire	5 + marquee: Board (max 20). Cabaret (max 100). Theatre (max 80). Reception (max 100).
Catering	Approved & self-catering.
Sleeps	18 S/C.
Closed	Never.
Directions	From Brecon, 4.5 miles west on A40 through Llanspyddid. Pass 2nd 'phone kiosk on left. Sign on right hand side of road.

Davina & Gavin Hogg
Brecon LD3 8EU
Tel   +44 (0)1874 636202
Email   penpont@btconnect.com
Web   www.penpont.com

Ethical Collection: Environment; Community; Food. See page 208 for details

Fairyhill Hotel

The Gower Peninsula has glorious heathland, a rugged coastline and some of the best beaches in the country. Fairyhill is bang in the middle of it all, a sublime country house wrapped up in 24 acres of peace. The billiard room overlooks the garden and is licensed for civil ceremonies, and there's a terrace with parkland views for lunch parties and weddings; the garden room is perfect for a small, intimate wedding breakfast. Inside glows with warmth and colour: find an open fire in the bar, a grand piano in the sitting room and informal spaces for your celebration. Come for private business meetings in rooms with surround sound and all the IT trimmings; there are break-out rooms too, with leather sofas and easy chairs. Super local food can be buffet style for meetings, three-course sit-down for weddings and parties. Comfortable bedrooms are big and fancy or small and sweet; some have painted beams, others have golden wallpaper, all have excellent bathrooms. Book a massage in the treatment room, play croquet, stroll down to a stream-fed lake, an ancient orchard, a walled garden. All is organised with flair.

Room hire	3: Board (max 16). Theatre (max 30). Reception (max 32).
Catering	In-house catering. Locally sourced.
Sleeps	16 B&B or DB&B.
Closed	First 3 weeks in January.
Directions	M4 junc. 47, A483 south, then A484 west to Gowerton and B4295 for Llanrhidian. Through Oldwalls, 1 mile up on left.

Andrew Hetherington & Paul Davies
Reynoldston, Swansea SA3 1BS

Tel	+44 (0)1792 390139
Email	postbox@fairyhill.net
Web	www.fairyhill.net

Entry 155   Map 2

Holm House

A glittering hotel down by the sea, a stylish, intimate and hugely spoiling spot for weddings, celebrations and meetings. Every square inch is covered with something lovely, so step into this grand Edwardian house and find half-panelled walls, vintage wallpaper, silk drapery and a mirrored bar. Interiors mix Art Deco touches with contemporary flair. Downstairs, doors everywhere open onto a balustraded terrace (al fresco dinners in summer) with formal gardens below and a sparkling sea beyond; on a good day you're on the Côte d'Azur. Drink in the view, still your mind for a brainstorming session then trip down to the beach for sailing lessons and boat trips. Slip into the airy restaurant for delicious working lunches and extravagant wedding breakfasts, where the focus is on excellent local produce: Welsh lamb, beef and cheeses. Beautiful bedrooms come with super beds, designer fabrics and Italian ceramics. Rooms at the back look out to sea, the best have balconies. There are loungers on a sun terrace, a spa for organic treatments and a hydrotherapy pool: pampering heaven for bridal parties!

Room hire	3: Board (max 20). Cabaret (max 50). Theatre (max 40).
Catering	In-house catering.
Sleeps	26 B&B or DB&B.
Closed	Never.
Directions	M4 junc. 33, then A4232 south. Follow signs to Penarth town centre (not marina). Along seafront, up hill, 1st right; 4th house on right.

Susan Sessions
Marine Parade, Penarth CF64 3BG

Tel	+44 (0)2920 701572
Email	info@holmhouse.co.uk
Web	www.holmhouse.co.uk

Scotland

Delgatie Castle

Mary Queen of Scots slept here in 1562. But this medieval castle with 11th-century keep forgoes airs and graces in favour of cosiness and intimacy. It's delightfully higgledy-piggledy inside, with studded oak doors, a turnpike staircase and countless nooks and crannies; and a history of similar twists and turns. How romantic to marry in the tiny old chapel or in the Yester Room next door, under a ceiling of heraldic shields. And to trip up to the Ballroom for an intimate dinner for 50, and dance amid panelled walls and high windows dressed in crimson damask. There's a Withdrawing Room to catch your breath in, and a Solar Room for smaller parties or meetings. Joan, who heads the castle's charitable trust, is passionate about Delgatie: she'll arrange shooting parties, craft workshops, concerts, corporate awaydays, you name it. Although the castle is open to the public every day, there are private apartments (with kitchens) on site, all yours from 4pm. Feeling outdoorsy? You can fish on the estate's loch, book a session of golf or stride out into Aberdeenshire's glorious countryside.

Room hire	3: Board (max 40). Cabaret (max 50). Theatre (max 80). Reception (max 50).
Catering	In-house catering.
Sleeps	28 S/C.
Closed	20 December-8 January.
Directions	Three miles north of Turriff off the B947 Banff to Aberdeen road.

Joan Johnson
Delgatie, Turriff AB53 5TD

Tel	+44 (0)1888 563479
Email	joan@delgatiecastle.com
Web	www.delgatiecastle.com

Kincardine Castle

The first sight of this castle takes your breath away. In 3000 acres, with superb views across the Dee valley, Kincardine was built by Andrew's family in the 1890s. It was designed for entertaining: the welcoming Great Hall, its wood panelling studded with stags heads, has a huge fireplace, grand piano and minstrels gallery, while the light airy drawing room and grand dining room, lavishly furnished, revels in incomparable views. Comfort and merriment are guaranteed in such majestic, yet mellow, surroundings. The décor and furniture of this family home reflect generations of collecting, from ancestral portraits to Jane Austen's ivory cup and ball, and bedrooms are as individual and as charming as all the rest; the Chinese room sports the only drum bed outside the V&A. Exclusive use of castle and grounds means everything, from cosy house parties to concerts to extravagant weddings, works brilliantly. Ceremonies are held in the grounds or in the castle, with room for marquees on any scale, a pretty walled garden for photos, and on summer evenings, pathways glowing with lanterns. *No civil licence.*

Room hire	4 + marquee: Board (max 30). Cabaret (max 56). Theatre (max 100). Reception (max 120).
Catering	In-house & own caterers.
Sleeps	25 DB&B.
Closed	Christmas & New Year; late July to early August.
Directions	From Aberdeen take A94 to Kincardine O'Neil. In village, lodge gates on right opposite school.

Andrew Bradford
Kincardine O'Neil, Aboyne AB34 5AE
Tel   +44 (0)1339 884225
Email   kincardineestate@btinternet.com
Web   www.kincardinecastle.com

Cavens

As you sweep south from Dumfries, the imperious Solway Firth looms before you – vast tracts of tidal sands besieged by birds, lush fields dotted with sheep, big skies hanging overhead. Inside this 1753 shooting lodge, quietly elegant rooms flood with light; it's a very pleasant place for parties, business meetings and small weddings. Choose your spot for the ceremony – Scottish ministers can tie the knot anywhere! The yellow dining room (which doubles as a fully-equipped board room) glows with a roaring fire. The less formal green room has plenty of comfortable sofas; the sitting room brims with busts and oils, floral curtains, fine china and a baby grand. The terrace overlooking the garden – views reach over sweeping lawns and native woods – is a grand place for bigger parties, and there's plenty of room for a marquee. You could bring your own caterers, but why bother? Food is a big draw here: local, seasonal, with vegetables fresh from the garden. Country-house bedrooms come with smart florals, mahogany dressers, bowls of fruit; some are snug, others palatial. Angus looks after everything impeccably.

Room hire	3 + marquee: Board (max 20). Cabaret (max 200). Theatre (max 20). Reception (max 200).
Catering	In-house & own caterers. Locally sourced.
Sleeps	22: 16 B&B or DB&B; 6 S/C.
Closed	Never.
Directions	From Dumfries, A710 to Kirkbean (12 miles). Cavens signed in village, on left.

Jane & Angus Fordyce
Kirkbean, Dumfries DG2 8AA

Tel	+44 (0)1387 880234
Email	enquiries@cavens.com
Web	www.cavens.com

Fenton Tower

Tall and proud in East Lothian's rolling countryside stands Fenton Tower: a 16th-century fortified tower and one-time refuge of King James VI of Scotland. Sacked by Oliver Cromwell, it has been magnificently restored as a venue for weddings, house parties, meetings and celebrations. Duck in through the pinkish exterior to confront Scottish drama: tapestries clothe walls, rich colours drip and drape, and a log fire roars in the cosy 'great hall'; guests may gather to sip a local malt. A suit of armour stands guard in the vaulted dining room, stunning in candlelight – it seats 32 but if your guest list goes over the top, just add a marquee. Meetings take place here or in the library; and you can marry, with notice for a licence. Spiral upwards over five floors to an array of beautifully restored bedrooms with every modern comfort (choose B&B or be pampered by a private chef), from which the views go on for miles. The outdoors are just as glorious. You're 20 miles from Edinburgh yet you can organise golf, shooting, fishing, stride North Berwick's deserted beaches, or daydream surrounded by the castle's laich.

Room hire	3 + marquee: Board (max 22). Cabaret (max 300). Theatre (max 40). Reception (max 300).
Catering	In-house catering.
Sleeps	12 B&B or catered house.
Closed	Rarely.
Directions	A1 from Edinburgh, take Abbotsview Junction, follow A199. Left onto B1347 to North Berwick for 4 miles. Tower on hill on right before Kingston.

Alan Thomson
Kingston, North Berwick EH39 5JH

Tel	+44 (0)1620 890089
Email	manager@fentontower.com
Web	www.fentontower.com

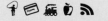

Bluebell Croft

Come for everything we love most – fine food, breathtaking views, bracing air, special people, green living – in a windswept croft in the remotest West Highlands. A ferry across Loch Linnhe, a stirring drive along the coast; then up, up a glacial valley, past tapestries of fields to a dramatic hilltop and snow-capped peaks. Your heart will sing as you prepare for your family gathering – or house party, residential course or wedding. You can marry in the garden, or in Honeysuckle House, inviting with its light open-plan ground floor, heaps of wood, a log stove, brick chimney and toasty Aga. Awake to birdsong and sunlight in cheery bedrooms with underfloor heating, invigorate achy muscles under powerful showers, soak in what must be Scotland's best-positioned hot tub, overlooking the mountains. Bill teaches home-smoking and Sukie (once Rural Chef of the Year) is a dab hand at events. She runs Aga cookery courses and rustles up mouthwatering meals from simple to five-course feasts using their own organic produce. There are lochs, woods and deserted beaches, so hike, cycle, kayak, fish. Heaven. *No marquees.*

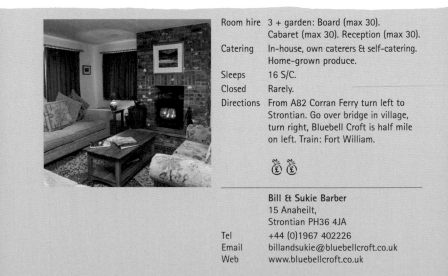

Room hire	3 + garden: Board (max 30). Cabaret (max 30). Reception (max 30).
Catering	In-house, own caterers & self-catering. Home-grown produce.
Sleeps	16 S/C.
Closed	Rarely.
Directions	From A82 Corran Ferry turn left to Strontian. Go over bridge in village, turn right, Bluebell Croft is half mile on left. Train: Fort William.

Bill & Sukie Barber
15 Anaheilt,
Strontian PH36 4JA

Tel	+44 (0)1967 402226
Email	billandsukie@bluebellcroft.co.uk
Web	www.bluebellcroft.co.uk

Entry 161   Map 8

Glenmorangie, The Highland Home at Cadboll

Glenmorangie – glen of tranquillity – and so it is. Bliss! Owned by the eponymous distillery, this 1700s farmhouse of thick walls and immaculate interiors stands in glorious countryside. A perfect place, a real find, with levels of service to surpass most others; staff are attentive yet unobtrusive, and the comforts are unremitting. It's a gorgeous backdrop for the perfect wedding or elegant party, and an exceptional hideaway for corporate get-togethers. Opportunities abound for relaxation after a hard day's work: golf at Royal Dornoch, sea fishing, dolphin-watching trips, and the distillery nearby. Celebrations for up to 30 guests can fan out in the house: find a crackling fire and plump sofas in the drawing room. Intimate house parties can expect fabulous dinners featuring local meat and seafood, and if you're throwing a big bash, opt for a marquee and a hog roast on the trim lawn. Stroll down a tree-lined path leading to a private beach, or explore the beautiful and productive walled garden. Bedrooms are sublime too: decanters of whisky, smart tartans, boundless country views.

Room hire	3 + marquee: Board (max 12). Cabaret (max 180). Theatre (max 12). Reception (max 180).
Catering	In-house & approved caterers.
Sleeps	18 DB&B.
Closed	January.
Directions	A9 north from Inverness for 33 miles to Nigg r'bout. Right on B9175, for Nigg, over r'way crossing for 1.5 miles, then left, following signs to house.

£££££

Martin Baxter
Fearn, Tain IV20 1XP

Tel	+44 (0)1862 871671
Email	relax@glenmorangie.co.uk
Web	www.theglenmorangiehouse.com

Greshornish House Hotel

How deeply romantic to marry here, under the boughs of the oldest laburnum tree on Skye! Or on the terrace overlooking tranquil Loch Greshornish. Lovely for a party, too – you can stay overnight – or a gathering of colleagues. It's difficult to imagine an environment more conducive to clear thinking than this slightly eccentric country house, remote, peaceful and approached along a single track road grazed by sheep. Have fun inside with a piano to play, a billiard table, a glowing fire, lots of books and heaps of sofas and chairs to unwind in. Outside are ten acres of woodland to explore, paths down to the loch where dolphins, seals and otters can be espied, and a croquet lawn. Neil and Rosemary are everywhere and run the place with infectious charm; take tea in the conservatory, look forward to delicious local food. Meals are buffet style or proper sit-down affairs with white tablecloths and fresh flowers, in a dining room with space to dance. Warm traditional bedrooms are mostly large, all with lovely water or garden views. Shut the rest of the world out: there is no mobile signal in the house!

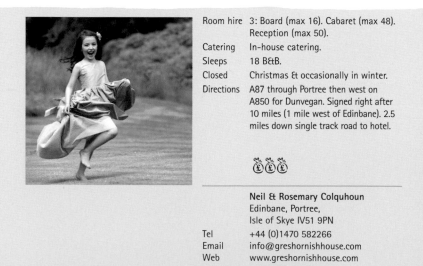

Room hire	3: Board (max 16). Cabaret (max 48). Reception (max 50).
Catering	In-house catering.
Sleeps	18 B&B.
Closed	Christmas & occasionally in winter.
Directions	A87 through Portree then west on A850 for Dunvegan. Signed right after 10 miles (1 mile west of Edinbane). 2.5 miles down single track road to hotel.

Neil & Rosemary Colquhoun
Edinbane, Portree,
Isle of Skye IV51 9PN

Tel +44 (0)1470 582266
Email info@greshornishhouse.com
Web www.greshornishhouse.com

Alexander House

Escape high into the Perthshire hills to a grandly sumptuous new house set magnificently against the mountains. Take family, friends, colleagues to celebrate a special occasion; kick back for a weekend; hold a get-away-from-it-all meeting. Sitting happily in the landscape, the house has been designed in traditional Scottish style and to the highest ecological specification; smart as smart can be, yet warm and cosy within. A wrought-iron chandelier greets you in the hall, a fire-warmed drawing room opens to valley views. Guests naturally gravitate to the vast, brilliantly light open-plan kitchen and sitting room, which expands outside through glass doors; relax with a local malt on a leather sofa. The place is all yours so cook if you feel inspired; otherwise book the caterers. Upstairs are bedrooms galore, each different, each super-comfy – there's even a four-poster and a lovers' bath. It's a playground for all ages, with a hot tub, a snooker table, a heated swimming pool, swings. All the traditional Scottish countryside pursuits are to hand, and Gleneagles is just down the road. Bring the boots!

Room hire	Whole house: Board (max 25). Cabaret (max 60). Reception (max 60).
Catering	Approved & self-catering.
Sleeps	20 S/C or catered. Extra beds.
Closed	Rarely.
Directions	From A9 exit for Gleneagles, then Duchally road for 3 miles. Turning on right. Gleneagles Station 10 minutes by taxi.

	Jo Lewis
	Auchterarder PH3 1PR
Tel	+44 (0)1420 85335
Email	info@alexanderhousescotland.com
Web	www.alexanderhousescotland.com

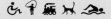

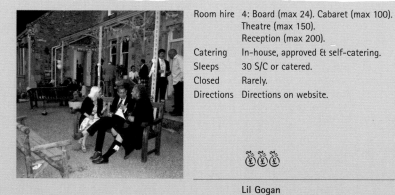

Kippilaw House

Meander down a tunnel of trees and land softly in three acres of stunning landscaped woodland garden. The Big Scottish Hoose (to quote the owners) is a large rambling Victorian mansion with 43 rooms and 34 fireplaces, crammed with vintage furniture and interesting knick-knacks. Imagine a house party: drinks in the chandelier'd Grand Hall; a speech from the landing; dinner around a candlelit table (perhaps with an impromptu piano performance); and you can loll on red velvet sofas in the fire-warmed Drawing Room. For a wedding or large party book the Ballroom; it opens to a south-facing veranda. In-house meals can be organised for up to 24, or caterers arranged, and if you hire the whole house the kitchen's yours. Bedrooms are vast and varied, with space to add more beds where needed. All except the master suite share bathrooms with claw-foot tubs and walk-in showers, one with a Victorian 'Thunder Box' loo! Laid-back and sociable, Lil and Douglas (both creative types) live in a separate wing and are always happy to help. This is a lovely informal place and you can really let your hair down.

Room hire	4: Board (max 24). Cabaret (max 100). Theatre (max 150). Reception (max 200).
Catering	In-house, approved & self-catering.
Sleeps	30 S/C or catered.
Closed	Rarely.
Directions	Directions on website.

Lil Gogan
Melrose TD6 9HF

Tel	+44 (0)1835 822790
Email	lilgogan@btopenworld.com
Web	www.kippilaw.com

Wedderburn Castle

Sweep through a lion-topped stone arch into immaculate parkland; the turreted Georgian façade — topped with battlements — is a showstopper. Inside, high windows flood vast rooms with light, picking out oodles of period detail: ornate plasterwork, stone fireplaces, beautiful furniture, burnished floors. Dramatic twin staircases lead from entrance hall to first-floor landing, the setting for small wedding ceremonies; guests look on from the minstrel's gallery. Subtle 21st-century additions to this 18th-century Borders castle include efficient central heating and lovely bathrooms. There are stunning views from a bevy of gracious and adaptable rooms, suitable for anything from a small meeting to a grand party: a chandeliered ballroom, a Wedgewood-blue morning room, a formal drawing room, a dining room. Spacious bedrooms are grand but homely; there are cottages too. Unwind in the billiard room and old kitchen below stairs, where a full-time chef is on hand to cater for everything, from receptions to weekend parties. Owner David has organised umpteen events here, and takes care of every detail. Enjoy!

Room hire	4: Board (max 44). Cabaret (max 92). Theatre (max 92). Reception (max 92).
Catering	In-house catering.
Sleeps	40: 26 B&B; 14 S/C.
Closed	Never.
Directions	From centre of Duns A6105 signed Berwick-upon-Tweed; on leaving Duns right turn to Wedderburn Castle (signed).

David Home
Duns TD11 3LT

Tel	+44 (0)1361 882190
Email	enquiries@wedderburncastle.com
Web	www.wedderburncastle.com

Ballochneck

This magical pile stands one mile up a private drive, soundproofed by 175 acres of lush Stirlingshire country. Swans nest on the lake in spring while Texel sheep graze the fields and deer roam the grounds. The house – still a home, albeit a grand one – dates to 1863 and if you're looking to host a smart, intimate wedding then look no further; if you top 40, opt for a marquee on the lawn. Nothing could be more romantic then getting wed under a fig tree amid beautifully tended rose bushes, beds of lavender and wandering clematis. And they'll happily do house parties, meetings, even conferences. Inside you get all the aristocratic works – roaring fires, painted panelling, magical windows that bring in the view, ornate ceilings. But Donnie and Fiona are the real stars; expect a few good stories and a trip to the top of the house where a full-size snooker table stands. This is shooting and stalking land, so there's Ballochneck pheasant and eggs, vegetables and herbs from the garden – it's foodie heaven. Vast bedrooms have huge views and beautiful beds; the best has an open fire. Charming.

Ethical Collection: Food.
See page 208 for details

Room hire	3 + marquee: Board (max 16). Cabaret (max 120). Theatre (max 40). Reception (max 120).
Catering	In-house & approved caterers.
Sleeps	6 B&B.
Closed	Christmas & New Year.
Directions	M9 junc. 10; A84 west, B8075 south, A811 to Buchlyvie. There, right onto B835 for Aberfoyle. Over bridge, up to lodge house 200 yds on left. 1 mile up drive.

Donnie & Fiona Allan
Buchlyvie, Stirling, FK8 3PA

Tel   +44 (0)1360 850216
Email   info@ballochneck.com
Web   www.ballochneck.com

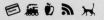

BELLA & FIFI
'FLORAL BONNES VIVANTES'
CORDIALLY INVITE

You, yes you!

TO CELEBRATE THE COMING TOGETHER OF

Enchanting Design
&
Ethical Beauty

WITH OUR DIVINE, LOCALLY SOURCED FLOWERS ON

Your special day
AT
A venue in this guide

RSVP BY CALLING US FOR A FREE
CONSULTATION ON **07505 841 528** OR VISIT
WWW.BELLAFIFIFLOWERS.CO.UK

Bella
&Fifi

Many of you may want to stay in environmentally friendly places. You may be passionate about local, organic or home-grown food. Or perhaps you want to know that the place you are staying in contributes to the community? To help you we have launched our Ethical Collection, so you can find the right place to stay and also discover how each owner is addressing these issues.

The Collection is made up of places going the extra mile, and taking the steps that most people have not yet taken, in one or more of the following areas:

• **Environment** Those making great efforts to reduce the environmental impact of their Special Place. We expect more than energy-saving light bulbs and recycling – in this part of the Collection you will find owners who make their own natural cleaning products, properties with solar hot water and biomass boilers, the odd green roof and a good measure of green elbow grease.

• **Community** Given to owners who use their property to play a positive role in their local and wider community. For example, by making a contribution from every guest's bill to a local fund, or running pond-dipping courses for local school children on their farm.

• **Food** Awarded to owners who make a real effort to source local or organic food, or to grow their own. We look

for those who have gone out of their way to strike up relationships with local producers or to seek out organic suppliers. It is easier for an owner on a farm to produce their own eggs than for someone in the middle of a city, so we take this into account.

How it works

To become part of our Ethical Collection owners choose whether to apply in one, two or all three categories, and fill in a detailed questionnaire asking demanding questions about their activities in the chosen areas. You can download a full list of the questions at www.sawdays.co.uk/about_us/ethical_collection/faq/

We then review each questionnaire carefully before deciding whether or not to give the award(s). The final decision is subjective; it is based not only on whether an owner ticks 'yes' to a question but also on the detailed explanation that accompanies each 'yes' or 'no' answer. For example, an owner who has tried as hard as possible to install solar water-heating panels, but has failed because of strict conservation planning laws, will be given some credit for their effort (as long as they are doing other things in this area).

We have tried to be as rigorous as possible and have made sure the questions are demanding. We have not checked out the claims of owners before making our decisions, but we do trust them to be honest. We are only human, as are they, so please let us know if you think we have made any mistakes.

The Ethical Collection is still a new initiative for us, and we'd love to know what you think about it – email us at ethicalcollection@sawdays.co.uk or write to us. And remember that because this is a new scheme some owners have not yet completed their questionnaires – we're sure other places in the guide are working just as hard in these areas, but we don't yet know the full details.

Ethical Collection online

There is stacks more information on our website, www.sawdays.co.uk. You can read the answers each owner has given to our Ethical Collection questionnaire and get a more detailed idea of what they are doing in each area. You can also search for properties that have awards.

Ethical Collection in this book

On the entry page of all places in the Collection we show which awards have been given.

A list of places in our Ethical Collection is shown below, by entry number.

Environment
5 • 15 • 26 • 32 • 35 • 37 • 53 • 54 • 66 • 67 • 77 • 80 • 85 • 94 • 95 • 114 • 116 • 130 • 131 • 154 • 164

Community
2 • 5 • 13 • 15 • 26 • 32 • 35 • 45 • 54 • 66 • 67 • 80 • 84 • 114 • 116 • 118 • 131 • 154

Food
5 • 9 • 15 • 26 • 32 • 35 • 45 • 53 • 54 • 67 • 77 • 80 • 85 • 94 • 95 • 114 • 116 • 130 • 131 • 154 • 164 • 167

Photo: The Pines Calyx, entry 80

Wheelchair–friendly
Wheelchair access to some
public rooms and to wcs.

England
Bath & N.E. Somerset 2
Berkshire 3 • 4
Birmingham 5
Bristol 7 • 8 • 9 • 11 • 12 • 14
Cornwall 16 • 17 • 19 • 20 •
21 • 23 • 24 • 25 • 27
Cumbria 30 • 32 • 33
Derbyshire 35 • 36
Devon 38 • 39 • 40 • 41 • 44 •
46 • 47 • 48 • 50 • 51 • 54
Dorset 55 • 56 • 60
Essex 62
Gloucestershire 63 • 65 • 66 •
67 • 68 • 71
Hampshire 74
Hertfordshire 77
Kent 80
Leicestershire 81
Liverpool 83
London 85 • 86 • 88 • 89
Norfolk 91 • 93
Northumberland 94
Nottinghamshire 96 • 97 • 98
Oxfordshire 101 • 102 • 103 • 104
Shropshire 105 • 106 • 108 • 109
Somerset 110 • 111 • 112 •
113 • 115 • 116 • 118
Staffordshire 119
Suffolk 120 • 124
Sussex 125 • 128 • 129
Warwickshire 130
Wiltshire 131 • 132 • 133 •
134 • 135 • 137
Yorkshire 139 • 141 • 142 •
143 • 144 • 145 • 146

Wales
Ceredigion 148 • 149
Pembrokeshire 151
Powys 153 • 154

Scotland
Aberdeenshire 157 • 158
Highland 161
Isle of Skye 163
Perth & Kinross 164
Scottish Borders 165

Price bands
Low

England
Bath & N.E. Somerset 2
Bristol 8 • 10 • 11 • 12 • 13 • 14
Cornwall 17 • 22
Cumbria 29 • 33 • 34
Derbyshire 35
Devon 37 • 38 • 47 • 52
Gloucestershire 65
Liverpool 83
London 84 • 87
Northumberland 94 • 95
Nottinghamshire 97 • 98
Somerset 114 • 118
Staffordshire 119
Wiltshire 131 • 132 • 135 • 137
Yorkshire 145

Wales
Ceredigion 148 • 149
Swansea 155

Scotland
Aberdeenshire 157
Dumfries & Galloway 159
Highland 161

Medium

England
Berkshire 3
Birmingham 5
Bristol 7 • 9
Cornwall 15 • 16 • 18 • 19 •
20 • 21 • 23 • 24 • 25 • 27
Cumbria 28
Devon 39 • 42 • 43 • 45 • 46 •
49 • 50 • 51 • 53

High

House parties

Quick reference indices

Team-building activities

Corporate events

Suitable for film/photo shoots

Quick reference indices

Quick reference indices

Wedding/event planner

Wales

Scotland

Shooting/fishing

England

Fireworks allowed

Quick reference indices

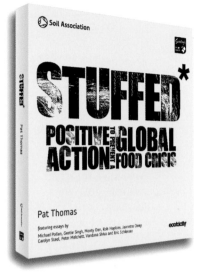

Stuffed – Postive Action to Prevent a Global Food Crisis   **£9.74**
                                                                (RRP £14.99)

Stuffed presents a global perspective on food production and agriculture with ideas for a fairly traded path we can follow to secure food for all and protection for the planet

With chapters on food in the kitchen through to global systems via the garden, schools, community, and an insight into food issues in cities and on farms, *Stuffed* takes a political and personal look the way that food systems influence, and can be influenced by, our choices.

Written by Patricia Thomas (former editor of The Ecologist), a preface by Michael Pollan, and with essays by Monty Don, Geetie Singh, Jeanette Orrey, Rob Hopkins, Carolyn Steel, Peter Melchett, Patrick Holden, Vandana Shiva and Eric Schlosser.

Also available in the Fragile Earth series:

Climate Change Our Warming World   £8.45 (RRP £12.99)
Money Matters Putting the eco into economics   £5.30 (RRP £7.99)
Do Humans Dream of Electric Cars?   £3.29 (RRP £4.99)
The Book of Rubbish Ideas   £4.54 (RRP £6.99)
The Big Earth Book Updated paperback edition   £8.45 (RRP £12.99)

To order any of the books in the Fragile Earth series call
+44 (0)1275 395431 or visit www.sawdays.co.uk/bookshop

Have you enjoyed this book? Why not try one of the others in the Special Places series and get 35% discount on the RRP *

British Bed & Breakfast (Ed 14)	RRP £14.99	Offer price £9.75
British Bed & Breakfast for Garden Lovers (Ed 5)	RRP £14.99	Offer price £9.75
British Hotels & Inns (Ed 11)	RRP £14.99	Offer price £9.75
Devon & Cornwall (Ed 1)	RRP £9.99	Offer price £6.50
Scotland (Ed 1)	RRP £9.99	Offer price £6.50
Wales (Ed 1)	RRP £9.99	Offer price £6.50
Pubs & Inns of England & Wales (Ed 7)	RRP £15.99	Offer price £9.75
Go Slow England	RRP £19.99	Offer price £13.00
Ireland (Ed 7)	RRP £12.99	Offer price £8.45
French Bed & Breakfast (Ed 11)	RRP £15.99	Offer price £10.40
French Self-catering (Ed 5)	RRP £14.99	Offer price £9.75
French Châteaux & Hotels (Ed 6)	RRP £14.99	Offer price £9.75
French Vineyards (Ed 1)	RRP £19.99	Offer price £13.00
Go Slow France	RRP £19.99	Offer price £13.00
Paris (Ed 1)	RRP £9.99	Offer price £6.50
Italy (Ed 6)	RRP £14.99	Offer price £9.75
Go Slow Italy	RRP £19.99	Offer price £13.00
Spain (Ed 8)	RRP £14.99	Offer price £9.75
Portugal (Ed 4)	RRP £11.99	Offer price £7.80
India & Sri Lanka (Ed 3)	RRP £11.99	Offer price £7.80
Green Europe (Ed 1)	RRP £11.99	Offer price £7.80
Morocco (Ed 3)	RRP £9.99	Offer price £9.10

*postage and packing is added to each order

To order at the Reader's Discount price simply phone +44 (0)1275 395431 and quote 'Reader Discount VEN'.

② Weddings • Parties • Meetings • Conferences   Somerset ①

Huntstile Organic Farm

③ Marry in the foothills of the Quantocks in a pretty marquee on the lawn; feast on delicious and beautifully presented food, much of it home-grown. For a rustic wedding in organic style on a working farm, John – born and bred here – can whisk you off to church in a flower-decked tractor-drawn trailer replete with straw bales, and back for a hog roast and a Ho-Down. There's a stone circle too, perfect for a hand-fasting ceremony. But this is not only a summer place: the Jacobean panelled farmhouse with its cosy log-fired dining room is lovely for winter parties and weddings too. Or come for a meeting or team-building day (complete with falconry workshop). There's sleeping room for family and friends in the welcoming old farmhouse (winding stairs for the nimble only) and in the smart modern Apple Loft and Cider House; or put up your tent in the camping field, where solar panel showers are fed from the farm's own spring. Wake to a wonderful breakfast (organic rashers, eggs from Lizzie's chickens). Huntstile Farm is an organic dream and Lizzie and John buzz with energy and enthusiasm. *No civil licence.*

④ Room hire	2 + marquee: Board (max 24). Cabaret (max 140). Theatre (max 160). Reception (max 140).	
⑤ Catering	In-house catering.	
⑥ Sleeps	28: 22 B&B; 6 S/C.	
⑦ Closed	End December–beginning January.	
⑧ Directions	M5 Junc. 24 , left at r'bout dir North Petherton. Follow signs for Goathurst & Broomfield, 2nd right to Goathurst. Huntstile 1 mile on right.	

⑨ 🐷 🐷

	Lizzie Myers
	Goathurst, Bridgwater TA5 2DQ
Tel	+44 (0)1278 662358
Email	huntstile@live.co.uk
Web	www.huntstileorganicfarm.co.uk

⑪ Ethical Collection: Environment; Community; Food. See page 208 for details

⑩ 🐷 🍴 🦮 🦅 🦌